JOSEPH
STALIN

JOSEPH STALIN

Dorothy and Thomas Hoobler

1985
CHELSEA HOUSE PUBLISHERS
NEW YORK

MANAGING EDITOR: William P. Hansen
ASSOCIATE EDITOR: John Haney
EDITORIAL COORDINATOR: Karyn Gullen Browne
EDITORIAL STAFF: Jennifer Caldwell
                 Richard Mandell
                 Susan Quist
ART DIRECTOR: Susan Lusk
ART ASSISTANTS: Teresa Clark, Carol McDougall
LAYOUT: Irene Friedman
COVER DESIGN: Mike Stromberg
PICTURE RESEARCH: Ellen Cibula

First Printing

Library of Congress Cataloging in Publication Data
Hoobler, Dorothy, and Hoobler, Thomas.
    Joseph Stalin.
    (World leaders past & present)
    Bibliography: p.
    Includes index.
    Summary: The life story of the revolutionary who became
leader of Communist Russia.
    1. Stalin, Joseph, 1879–1953—Juvenile literature.
2. Heads of state—Soviet Union—Biography—Juvenile
literature. [1. Stalin, Joseph, 1879–1953. 2. Heads of
state]   I. Hoobler, Thomas.   II. Title.   III. Series.
DK268.S8H66 1985   947.084′2′0924   [B] [92]   84–27457
ISBN 0-87754-576-6

Chelsea House Publishers
Harold Steinberg, Chairman & Publisher
Susan Lusk, Vice President
A Division of Chelsea House Educational Communications, Inc.

Chelsea House Publishers
133 Christopher Street
New York, N.Y. 10014

Photos courtesy of United Press International and The Bettmann Archive

CHELSEA HOUSE PUBLISHERS

WORLD LEADERS PAST & PRESENT

ADENAUER
ALEXANDER THE GREAT
MARK ANTONY
KING ARTHUR
KEMAL ATATÜRK
CLEMENT ATTLEE
BEGIN
BEN GURION
BISMARCK
LEON BLUM
BOLÍVAR
CESARE BORGIA
BRANDT
BREZHNEV
CAESAR
CALVIN
CASTRO
CATHERINE THE GREAT
CHARLEMAGNE
CHIANG KAI-SHEK
CHOU EN-LAI
CHURCHILL
CLEMENCEAU
CLEOPATRA
CORTEZ
CROMWELL
DANTON
DE GAULLE
DE VALERA
DISRAELI
EISENHOWER
ELEANOR OF AQUITAINE
QUEEN ELIZABETH I
FERDINAND AND ISABELLA

FRANCO
FREDERICK THE GREAT
INDIRA GANDHI
GANDHI
GARIBALDI
GENGHIS KHAN
GLADSTONE
HAMMARSKJÖLD
HENRY VIII
HENRY OF NAVARRE
HINDENBURG
HITLER
HO CHI MINH
KING HUSSEIN
IVAN THE TERRIBLE
ANDREW JACKSON
JEFFERSON
JOAN OF ARC
POPE JOHN XXIII
LYNDON JOHNSON
BENITO JUÁREZ
JFK
KENYATTA
KHOMEINI
KHRUSHCHEV
MARTIN LUTHER KING
KISSINGER
LENIN
LINCOLN
LLOYD GEORGE
LOUIS XIV
LUTHER
JUDAS MACCABEUS

MAO
MARY, QUEEN OF SCOTS
GOLDA MEIR
METTERNICH
MUSSOLINI
NAPOLEON
NASSER
NEHRU
NERO
NICHOLAS II
NIXON
NKRUMAH
PERICLES
PERÓN
QADDAFI
ROBESPIERRE
ELEANOR ROOSEVELT
FDR
THEODORE ROOSEVELT
SADAT
SUN YAT-SEN
STALIN
TAMERLAINE
THATCHER
TITO
TROTSKY
TRUDEAU
TRUMAN
QUEEN VICTORIA
WASHINGTON
CHAIM WEIZMANN
WOODROW WILSON
XERXES

Further titles in preparation

Contents

ON LEADERSHIP

Arthur M. Schlesinger, jr.

LEADERSHIP, it may be said, is really what makes the world go round. Love no doubt smooths the passage; but love is a private transaction between consenting adults. Leadership is a public transaction with history. The idea of leadership affirms the capacity of individuals to move, inspire and mobilize masses of people so that they act together in pursuit of an end. Sometimes leadership serves good purposes, sometimes bad; but whether the end is benign or evil, great leaders are those men and women who leave their personal stamp on history.

Now, the very concept of leadership implies the proposition that individuals can make a difference. This proposition has never been universally accepted. From classical times to the present day, eminent thinkers have regarded individuals as no more than the agents and pawns of larger forces, whether the gods and goddesses of the ancient world or, in the modern era, race, class, nation, the dialectic, the will of the people, the spirit of the times, history itself. Against such forces, the individual dwindles into insignificance.

So contends the thesis of historical determinism. Tolstoy's great novel *War and Peace* offers a famous statement of the case. Why, Tolstoy asked, did millions of men in the Napoleonic wars, denying their human feelings and their common sense, move back and forth across Europe slaughtering their fellows? "The war," Tolstoy answered, "was bound to happen simply because it was bound to happen." All prior history predetermined it. As for leaders, they, Tolstoy said, "are but the labels that serve to give a name to an end and, like labels, they have the least possible connection with the event." The greater the leader, "the more conspicuous the inevitability and the predestination of every act he commits." The leader, said Tolstoy, is "the slave of history."

Determinism takes many forms. Marxism is the determinism of class, Nazism the determinism of race. But the idea of men and women as the slaves of history runs athwart the deepest human instincts. Rigid determinism abolishes the idea of human freedom—the assumption of free choice that underlies every move we make, every word we speak, every thought we think. It abolishes the idea of human responsibility, since it is manifestly unfair to reward or punish people for actions that are by definition beyond their control. No one can live consistently by any deterministic creed. The Marxist states prove this themselves by their extreme susceptibility to the cult of leadership.

More than that, history refutes the idea that individuals make no difference. In December 1931 a British politician crossing Park Avenue in New York City between 76th and 77th Streets around ten-thirty at night looked in the wrong direction and was knocked down by an automobile—a moment, he later recalled, of a man aghast, a world aglare: "I do not understand why I was not broken like an eggshell or squashed like a gooseberry." Fourteen months later an American politician, sitting in an open car in Miami, Florida, was fired on by an assassin; the man beside him was hit. Those who believe that individuals make no difference to history might well ponder whether the next two decades would have been the same had Mario Contasini's car killed Winston Churchill in 1931 and Giuseppe Zangara's bullet killed Franklin Roosevelt in 1933. Suppose, in addition, that Adolf Hitler had been killed in the street fighting during the Munich *Putsch* of 1923 and that Lenin had died of typhus during the First World War. What would the 20th century be like now?

For better or for worse, individuals do make a difference. "The notion that a people can run itself and its affairs anonymously," wrote the philosopher William James, "is now well known to be the silliest of absurdities. Mankind does nothing save through initiatives on the part of inventors, great or small, and imitation by the rest of us—these are the sole factors in human progress. Individuals of genius show the way, and set the patterns, which common people then adopt and follow."

Leadership, James suggests, means leadership in thought as well as in action. In the long run, leaders in thought may well make the greater difference to the world. But, as Woodrow Wilson once said, "Those only are leaders of men, in the general eye, who lead in action. . . . It is at their hands that new thought gets its translation into the crude language of deeds." Leaders in thought often invent in solitude and obscurity, leaving to later generations the tasks of imitation. Leaders in action—the leaders portrayed in this series—have to be effective in their own time.

And they cannot be effective by themselves. They must act in response to the rhythms of their age. Their genius must be adapted, in a phrase of William James's, "to the receptivities of the moment." Leaders are useless without followers. "There goes the mob," said the French politician hearing a clamor in the streets. "I am their leader. I must follow them." Great leaders turn the inchoate emotions of the mob to purposes of their own. They seize on the opportunities of their time, the hopes, fears, frustrations, crises, potentialities.

They succeed when events have prepared the way for them, when the community is waiting to be aroused, when they can provide the clarifying and organizing ideas. Leadership ignites the circuit between the individual and the mass and thereby alters history.

It may alter history for better or for worse. Leaders have been responsible for the most extravagant follies and most monstrous crimes that have beset suffering humanity. They have also been vital in such gains as humanity has made in individual freedom, religious and racial tolerance, social justice and respect for human rights.

There is no sure way to tell in advance who is going to lead for good and who for evil. But a glance at the gallery of men and women in *World Leaders—Past and Present* suggests some useful tests.

One test is this: do leaders lead by force or by persuasion? By command or by consent? Through most of history leadership was exercised by the divine right of authority. The duty of followers was to defer and to obey. "Theirs not to reason why,/ Theirs but to do and die." On occasion, as with the so-called "enlightened despots" of the 18th century in Europe, absolutist leadership was animated by humane purposes. More often, absolutism nourished the passion for domination, land, gold and conquest and resulted in tyranny.

The great revolution of modern times has been the revolution of equality. The idea that all people should be equal in their legal condition has undermined the old structures of authority, hierarchy and deference. The revolution of equality has had two contrary effects on the nature of leadership. For equality, as Alexis de Tocqueville pointed out in his great study *Democracy in America*, might mean equality in servitude as well as equality in freedom.

"I know of only two methods of establishing equality in the political world," Tocqueville wrote. "Rights must be given to every citizen, or none at all to anyone . . . save one, who is the master of all." There was no middle ground "between the sovereignty of all and the absolute power of one man." In his astonishing prediction of 20th-century totalitarian dictatorship, Tocqueville explained how the revolution of equality could lead to the "*Führerprinzip*" and more terrible absolutism than the world had ever known.

But when rights are given to every citizen and the sovereignty of all is established, the problem of leadership takes a new form, becomes more exacting than ever before. It is easy to issue commands and enforce them by the rope and the stake, the concentration camp and the *gulag*. It is much harder to use argument and achievement to overcome opposition and win consent. The Founding Fathers of the United States understood the difficulty. They believed that history had given them the opportunity to decide, as

Alexander Hamilton wrote in the first Federalist Paper, whether men are indeed capable of basing government on "reflection and choice, or whether they are forever destined to depend . . . on accident and force."

Government by reflection and choice called for a new style of leadership and a new quality of followership. It required leaders to be responsive to popular concerns, and it required followers to be active and informed participants in the process. Democracy does not eliminate emotion from politics; sometimes it fosters demagoguery; but it is confident that, as the greatest of democratic leaders put it, you cannot fool all of the people all of the time. It measures leadership by results and retires those who overreach or falter or fail.

It is true that in the long run despots are measured by results too. But they can postpone the day of judgment, sometimes indefinitely, and in the meantime they can do infinite harm. It is also true that democracy is no guarantee of virtue and intelligence in government, for the voice of the people is not necessarily the voice of God. But democracy, by assuring the rights of opposition, offers built-in resistance to the evils inherent in absolutism. As the theologian Reinhold Niebuhr summed it up, "Man's capacity for justice makes democracy possible, but man's inclination to injustice makes democracy necessary."

A second test for leadership is the end for which power is sought. When leaders have as their goal the supremacy of a master race or the promotion of totalitarian revolution or the acquisition and exploitation of colonies or the protection of greed and privilege or the preservation of personal power, it is likely that their leadership will do little to advance the cause of humanity. When their goal is the abolition of slavery, the liberation of women, the enlargement of opportunity for the poor and powerless, the extension of equal rights to racial minorities, the defense of the freedoms of expression and opposition, it is likely that their leadership will increase the sum of human liberty and welfare.

Leaders have done great harm to the world. They have also conferred great benefits. You will find both sorts in this series. Even "good" leaders must be regarded with a certain wariness. Leaders are not demigods; they put on their trousers one leg after another just like ordinary mortals. No leader is infallible, and every leader needs to be reminded of this at regular intervals. Irreverence irritates leaders but is their salvation. Unquestioning submission corrupts leaders and demeans followers. Making a cult of a leader is always a mistake. Fortunately hero worship generates its own antidote. "Every hero," said Emerson, "becomes a bore at last."

The signal benefit the great leaders confer is to embolden the rest of us to live according to our own best selves, to be active, insistent, and resolute in affirming our own sense of things. For great leaders attest to the reality of human freedom against the supposed inevitabilities of history. And they attest to the wisdom and power that may lie within the most unlikely of us, which is why Abraham Lincoln remains the supreme example of great leadership. A great leader, said Emerson, exhibits new possibilities to all humanity. "We feed on genius. . . . Great men exist that there may be greater men."

Great leaders, in short, justify themselves by emancipating and empowering their followers. So humanity struggles to master its destiny, remembering with Alexis de Tocqueville: "It is true that around every man a fatal circle is traced beyond which he cannot pass; but within the wide verge of that circle he is powerful and free; as it is with man, so with communities."

—*New York*

1

The Making of a Revolutionary

To gain a victory and be feared was a triumph for him.
—ROBERT C. TUCKER
leading historian, on Stalin as a child

In December 1929 the Soviet Union celebrated the 50th birthday of its *vozhd*, or leader, Joseph Stalin. The nationwide celebration, with accolades in every city and village throughout the country, symbolized Stalin's control over the nation. He had beaten out numerous rivals to attain the position he now held. His power over Soviet life was absolute— and he would keep it until his death 24 years later.

Thousands of letters of congratulation poured into the Kremlin, the center of Soviet leadership. They came from officials and from ordinary citizens. Parades and performances were dedicated to Stalin's honor. A special issue of *Pravda*, the national newspaper, sang Stalin's praise in extravagant terms. He was called "beloved leader," "great and remarkable genius," "man of steel," and "granite Bolshevik."

Even in the prison camps of Siberia, inmates praised the leader who was responsible for their being there. It was a tribute that far outshone any of the opulent ceremonies of the tsars, the rulers of Russia before the Communist Revolution.

Professing modesty, Stalin published a reply to

A portrait of Joseph Stalin dating from the early 1930s, when the first Five Year Plan for Soviet economic growth was well under way and the forced collectivization of agriculture had begun radically to alter the lives of millions of Soviet peasants.

Joseph Stalin (at lower right) and classmates at the church school in Gori, Georgia, in 1892.

this tribute on *Pravda*'s front page. He accepted his honors as a representative of the Communist Party. He ended with, "Comrades, you need have no doubt that I am prepared in the future, too, to devote to the cause of the working class, to the cause of the proletarian revolution and world communism, all my strength, all my ability, and, if need be, all my blood, drop by drop."

Who was Stalin—the object of such acclaim? He was not prepossessing in appearance. He was only about five feet, four inches tall, although he wore specially built boots to increase his height. His face was heavily pockmarked from a childhood case of smallpox—although most Soviet citizens did not know that, since every photograph of him was re-touched to hide this defect.

His dark hair and thick, black moustache were typical of the Georgian peasants who were his ancestors. His low forehead framed eyes that have been described as warm brown to yellow. He usu-ally dressed in a plain khaki military tunic and trousers tucked into black leather boots.

Yet to him fell the role of leader of the largest nation in the world—covering fully one-sixth of the land area of the globe. His power was as great as any leader in world history. He had come a long way from his humble origins.

He was born Joseph Vissarionovich Dzhugashvili on December 21, 1879, in Gori, Georgia, a moun-tain town of about 5,000 people. Georgia was part of the vast Russian Empire. Like many sections of the empire, it had its own language and culture. It was located in the Caucasus, a mountainous re-gion between the Black Sea and the Caspian Sea. From early times Georgia was a crossroads between Asia and Europe. Within a few miles of his village, young Joseph could hear the sounds of many languages.

He was the only surviving son of Vissarion Dzhugashvili and Catherine Geladze. His father was a cobbler and by all accounts a brutal man given to drinking bouts and beating his son and wife. A childhood friend wrote that he never saw the boy

> *The working class? I know of no such class in Russia, Sergei Yulevich, I do not understand what you are talking about. We have peasants. They form ninety percent of the population. . . . You are trying to create artificially a new class, a sort of social relationship completely alien to Russia. In this respect, Sergei Yulevich, you are a dangerous socialist.*
>
> —K. P. POBEDONOSTSEV
> leading Russian churchman, to Count Sergei Yulevich Witte, the innovative but essentially conservative finance minister, around 1900

cry. He added, "Those undeserved and fearful beatings made the boy as hard and heartless as his father." Vissarion died in a brawl when his son was only 11.

Joseph was devoted to his mother. She took in laundry and sewing to support the family. She was a pious woman who took her son regularly to the village church where he sang in the choir. Her great hope for her Soso ("Joe") was that he would get a good education and become a priest of the Orthodox church. Years later, when he became ruler of the Soviet Union, she is said to have told him that he would have done better to become a priest.

Three other children in the family died in infancy. Stalin survived both the smallpox that scarred his face and an infection of the left elbow which left that arm shorter than his right. Stalin later recalled that this affliction left him close to death. What saved him was either a "healthy organism or

Horsedrawn artillery formations race through Moscow's Red Square during the 1928 May Day celebrations. Although the Red Army underwent extensive modernization during the 1930s, mainly at the instigation of the brilliant Marshal Tukhachevsky (whom Stalin had shot for alleged treason in 1937), horses still formed an important element of the Soviets' military transport capability in World War II.

. . . the ointments smeared on it by the village quack, but I got my health back."

Soso enrolled in the village school when he was eight. He was an able pupil and was at the top of his class. He read numerous books which glorified the Georgian past. Georgia had been independent before it was conquered by the Russian tsars.

One book that had a particularly deep effect on the boy had a character named Koba. Koba was a kind of Georgian Robin Hood. He hated the Russians and avenged their crimes against the Georgians. Koba's deeds were particularly ruthless and bloody. Stalin began to call himself Koba and was delighted when his friends took up the nickname.

Later he was to take Koba as his revolutionary pseudonym when he was hiding from the tsar's police.

By 1894 Soso had received all the schooling that was available in Gori, but he won a scholarship to the theological seminary in Tiflis, the capital of Georgia.

The theological seminary was a dark and gloomy stone building. The students were allowed no pri-

A Georgian monk of the Russian Orthodox faith. Stalin's education at the hands of such men only served to inflame his revolutionary tendencies. The Georgian clergy and the tsarist schools inspectorate denied the seminarians access to the works of Georgian national authors and Russian writers such as Turgenev and Tolstoy who consistently criticized the tsarist social order.

What a pity you never became a priest.

—CATHERINE GELADZE
Stalin's mother, speaking in 1936

vate life. The Russian monks who ran the seminary treated them like prisoners, spying on them and checking their rooms to see what they were reading. Each day was carefully scheduled. Study and prayer alternated. Students had only one short break in the afternoon, when they could take a supervised walk around the city.

At first, Stalin seemed to fit into the strict regimen. He did well in his schoolwork and received the highest mark for conduct. He found time to write nationalistic and romantic poems, which were published in a magazine devoted to the preservation of Georgian culture.

But Stalin's spirit chafed under the harsh regime. Years later, he told an interviewer, "In protest against the outrageous . . . methods prevalent in the seminary, I was ready to become, and actually did become, a revolutionary."

In 1898 Stalin took his first step to a revolutionary career when he joined a Marxist group in Tiflis. Fifty years earlier the German philosopher Karl Marx had published his *Communist Manifesto*.

Basically, Marx saw history as a succession of "class struggles" in which those who were economically productive took power from those who lived off the fruits of other people's work. Marx foresaw a final struggle which would result in a "classless society." In this society all people would share equally the fruits of their work.

According to Marx, the most recent struggle had seen capitalists (the "bourgeoisie") overthrow feudal barons. The stage was set for the final revolution between the bourgeoisie and the "proletariat," or industrial workers.

The group that Stalin first joined merely met to discuss Marx's ideas. Even in this intellectual atmosphere, Stalin would fly into a rage if the others disagreed with anything he said.

He soon passed from discussion and began a double life, slipping out of the seminary to secret meetings with working men at night. That summer he spent his vacation in Tiflis spreading Marxist ideas among workers. By the time the fall term began he had lost all interest in his studies.

When Stalin did not show up for his examinations, he was expelled from the seminary. A friend said that "he took with him a ferocious and enduring hatred against the college administration, against the bourgeoisie, against everything in the country that embodied tsarism. He had an overwhelming hatred against all authority."

Stalin, then 19 years old, remained in Tiflis, earning enough to live on by tutoring students. At the end of the year he got a job at the Tiflis Observatory. In the evenings he went to the railroad yards to talk with the workers about Marxism. He seems to have been successful at propagandizing, or spreading his political ideas. He helped to organize Tiflis's first May Day celebration in 1900. The celebration, held at a secret spot outside of town, was a peaceful one. The workers unfurled red banners, the symbol of revolution, sang songs, and listened to a few brief speeches.

The year that followed was a crucial one in Stalin's career. He met a member of the Social Democratic Party, and soon became a member.

The Russian Social Democratic Party was founded in 1898. Its members were socialists dedicated to putting Marxist ideas into practice. One of the leaders of the party was Vladimir Lenin, a lawyer whose brother had been executed for plotting against the tsar. After a term of exile in Siberia for his own activities, Lenin had left Russia to write and to plan a socialist revolution. Lenin was to become Stalin's hero.

At first, Stalin's party activities were confined to writing a few articles for *Brdzola* (*The Struggle*), an illegal Marxist magazine. He was helping plan a second May Day celebration when the tsarist police began a crackdown on the organizers. Stalin escaped the police roundup, and the party sent him to Batum for safety and to organize workers. This was a point of no return for Stalin; from now on he was a wanted man, a committed revolutionary known as Koba.

Batum was a city of about 30,000 people, mostly Turkish in heritage, on the Black Sea. It was important as an oil depot for the wells around the

A wooden chapel of the Russian Orthodox Church in the Soviet Union's Carpathian Mountains. Stalin's attendance at the Tiflis theological seminary placed him in the mainstream of the politics of dissent in Georgia. Many seminarians held nationalist views and were violently opposed to the Church hierarchy and to the tsarist officials who regulated the Church.

Tsarist policemen raid a Nihilist printing press in St. Petersburg during the 1890s. Many Russian revolutionaries of the late 19th century called themselves Nihilists. The word first appeared in *Fathers and Sons,* a novel by Ivan Turgenev (1818-1883), and was used to describe the hero of the story, Bazarov, a man dedicated to the complete annihilation of governmental authority.

Caspian Sea. Stalin helped organize a strike that led to a violent confrontation between workers and police. Fourteen people were killed, more injured, and over 500 workers were arrested.

Shortly afterward, the tsarist police arrested Stalin. He was in prison for a year and a half and then given a three-year exile in Siberia. The isolated, barren Siberian region was then, as now, used as a place of exile for political prisoners. They were not kept under guard, because the harsh conditions and isolation were regarded as sufficient punishment.

During Stalin's exile, a split took place in the Social Democratic Party. In a meeting in 1903, the members hotly debated what the role of the party should be. Should it be a traditional political party with membership open to any who were sympathetic? Or should it be a close-knit body of committed, full-time revolutionaries? Those who favored the more traditional course were termed Mensheviks. Those who espoused the revolutionary course were called Bolsheviks. Lenin was the leader of the Bolshevik faction.

Stalin escaped from Siberia and returned to Tiflis in 1904. Most of the Social Democrats in the Caucasus were Mensheviks. Stalin threw his lot in with the Bolsheviks. His decision was not surprising, since he was already a full-time revolutionary. The role of Lenin as leader of the revolutionary faction appealed to Stalin's personality, even though the two had not yet met.

In Tiflis, Stalin acted as if the real struggle were against the Mensheviks. A Menshevik and former

The city of Tiflis, capital of the Soviet republic of Georgia. Although the Soviet government recognized Georgia's independence soon after the Russian Revolution, Stalin's hatred of the country's moderate socialist government provoked him to order the invasion and annexation of his native land in 1921.

Karl Marx (1818-1883), the German political philosopher and founder of modern socialism. Expelled from Germany in 1849 for publishing his revolutionary opinions, Marx settled in London. Here, in 1895, his colleague Friedrich Engels (1820-1895) brought to completion the final volume of *Das Kapital*, Marx's massive treatise concerning politics and economics.

friend recalled, "He attacked us at every meeting . . . in the most savage and unscrupulous manner, trying to sow poison and hatred against us everywhere. He would have liked to root us out with fire and sword. . . . But the overwhelming majority of Georgian Marxists remained with us. That only angered and enraged him the more."

In 1905 revolution did break out in Russia. However, it resulted not from the agitation of professional revolutionaries, but from the people's anger at a war Russia was losing to Japan. The tsar's troops fired upon a demonstration in the capital city, St. Petersburg. Almost at once, spontaneous risings took place throughout Russia.

In the Caucasus, Stalin organized demonstrations and strikes, but the real action was in the two largest cities, Moscow and St. Petersburg. In both of these, the Social Democrats organized *soviets*, or workers' councils, to coordinate actions against the tsar's regime.

The leader of the St. Petersburg soviet was Leon Trotsky. A flamboyant orator and political writer, Trotsky had backed the Mensheviks in the party split of 1903. Since then, he had taken on a conciliatory role, trying to bring the two factions together. Trotsky was to become Stalin's great enemy within the party.

The 1905 revolution was put down with a combination of compromise and force. Trotsky and most of the rest of the soviet members were arrested. But the tsar was forced to grant the election of a parliament, known as the Duma.

The Social Democrats met to discuss the situation. Stalin traveled to Tammerfors, Finland (then part of the Russian Empire), for the meeting. Here he met Lenin for the first time. Stalin's description of Lenin is interesting for what it says about Stalin:

"I was expecting to see the mountain eagle of our party, a great man, not only politically, but if you will, physically, for I had formed for myself an image of Lenin as a giant, stately and imposing. What was my disappointment when I saw the most ordinary-looking man, below middle height, distinguished from ordinary mortals by nothing, literally nothing."

Some party members felt they should participate in the democratic process and campaign for membership in the Duma. Others insisted that Marxist theory demanded they disdain such "bourgeois" institutions, and work for revolution.

The dispute carried over to the next party congress, in Stockholm in 1906. This was Stalin's first trip outside the Russian Empire. One of the questions raised at the congress was embarrassing to him. This was the matter of revolutionary expropriations, or "exes." "Exes" were criminal acts such as hijackings and bank robberies used to raise funds for the party.

In Georgia, the key leader of the "exes" was a friend of Stalin. Stalin helped plan some illegal acts, but did not take part in them. Nevertheless, he was stung when both factions of the party declared their opposition to such activities. Lenin won Stalin's admiration by refusing to condemn the "exes." In his view, any means of raising party funds was acceptable.

It was here that Stalin's animosity toward the intellectuals of the party began. Many party leaders lived outside Russia, safe from the tsar's police, writing about the theory of revolution. Stalin felt he was doing the real work, the practice of revolution, risking his skin inside Russia.

The following year, at another party congress, Stalin met Trotsky for the first time. Trotsky had just escaped from a lifetime sentence in Siberia for his role in the St. Petersburg soviet. The attention given to Trotsky at the congress aroused Stalin's jealousy. Trotsky's outspokenness in condemning "exes" further irritated Stalin.

In an article about the congress, Stalin described Trotsky as a case of "beautiful uselessness." At a later meeting, in 1913, Trotsky noticed the "glint of animosity" in Stalin's "yellow eyes." But he dismissed Stalin as a "mediocrity."

The period was a time of personal tragedy for Stalin. Around 1903 he had married a young Geor-

Seminarian Joseph Stalin in 1895. The theological seminary in Tiflis, which Joseph attended from 1894 to 1899, had a reputation as a hotbed of political dissent. In 1886 a seminarian named Joseph Laghiashvili shot the Russian rector of the school and became a national hero following his execution.

Leading Russian revolutionary Vladimir Lenin (at center) and members of the St. Petersburg League for the Liberation of the Working Class. The picture was taken shortly before Lenin's arrest by the tsarist police on December 20, 1895. Lenin spent 1896 in a Petrograd prison, secretly working on a book entitled *The Development of Capitalism in Russia.*

gian woman named Catherine Svanidze. Theirs was a traditional Georgian marriage with the husband as dominant partner, rather than a marriage of equals as Marxist thought called for.

A friend wrote of the marriage, "It was not in his character to feel any sense of equality with anyone. His marriage was a happy one because his wife . . . regarded him as a demigod, and because, being a Georgian woman, she was brought up in the sacrosanct tradition that a woman is born to serve."

His wife, like his mother, was a devout Orthodox Christian. She prayed for Joseph to change his revolutionary ways. She worried as he left for his secret meetings, always hoping she would see him again.

But Stalin seems to have truly loved her, and when she died at an early age, in 1907, her husband pointed to her coffin and said, "She was the one creature who softened my heart of stone. She is dead, and with her have died my last warm feelings for humanity." Pointing to his heart, he said, "It is all so desolate here, so inexpressibly empty." These are the most human words that Stalin ever spoke.

Stalin returned to the Caucasus, working in the city of Baku on the Caspian Sea. It was the center of the developing Russian oil industry. By this time revolutionary activity in the rest of Russia had died down. In Baku, however, Stalin and others succeeded in organizing a general strike in the spring of 1908.

The strike drew the attention of the rest of the socialist movement. Lenin approvingly called the Baku workers "our last Mohicans of the political mass strike." But Stalin paid a price for his success—the tsar's police again arrested and imprisoned him. He was exiled to the far north.

> *They are systematic and persistent in the pursuits of bad ends. But their chief method is surveillance, spying, invasion of the inner life, the violation of people's feelings, and what can be positive in that?*
> —JOSEPH STALIN
> speaking of his seminary teachers

Striking St. Petersburg workers flee as the tsar's troops fire on them, January 9, 1905. The demonstrators, led by a liberal priest named George Gapon, had intended to ask Tsar Nicholas II to intervene in a factory dispute between management and workers.

Russian infantry in Manchuria await a Japanese advance during the Russian-Japanese War (1904-1905). The military shortcomings and general illiteracy of the Russian recruits were in marked contrast to the skill and intelligence shown by the Japanese, who had greatly benefited from the universal elementary and secondary education which had been available to all classes of society in Japan since 1860.

Between 1909 and 1917, Stalin spent most of his time in prison or exile. It was a lonely life. The revolutionary fervor of the nation had waned, and the party membership dropped drastically.

Stalin kept in touch with the party leadership abroad. At the party conference in Prague in 1912 he was named a member of the central committee, the decision-making body of the party. This was a great honor, and it was Lenin who was responsible for the promotion. With Lenin's backing, Stalin took on more important tasks. He helped to found the newspaper *Pravda* and wrote for it when he was not in prison.

In 1913 Joseph, or Koba, began to use the revolutionary name Stalin. Taken from the Russian word

Mounted policemen charge a crowd of striking workers in St. Petersburg in January 1905. The brutality of the official reaction to the workers' demonstrations destroyed Tsar Nicholas II's prospects of political survival. Many workers became increasingly aware of the injustices inherent in the tsarism.

Leon Trotsky (1877-1940), the eminent Russian communist who played a leading role in the Russian Revolution and was subsequently appointed commissar for foreign affairs.

A Russian landowner announcing emancipation to his serfs in 1856. The fact that Russia had barely emerged from feudalism by the late 19th century greatly contributed to the violent opposition to Russian society offered by such revolutionaries as Stalin, whose education made him aware of the extent to which Russia had lagged behind the other nations of Europe.

The Georgian city of Baku, where Stalin's return from exile in Siberia in 1909 received much attention from other revolutionaries. Stalin complained that the revolutionary leadership had insufficient understanding of the true political situation inside Russia.

Tsar Alexander II (1818-1881), the Russian ruler whose 1856 emancipation of the serfs (slaves) did not prevent continued social unrest throughout the 1860s and 1870s.

for "steel," the name seemed singularly appropriate. He was to show his steel-like qualities in many ways, and the name also symbolized his growing identification as a Russian, rather than a Georgian.

The longest unbroken period of his exile was between 1913 and 1917. In the freezing, barren wasteland of the Russian north, other exiles wasted away physically and mentally. For Stalin it was a time of tempering, when the final cast of his character was formed.

A man who knew him in exile said, "He usually remained taciturn and morose, placidly smoking his pipe. . . . Neither was there any personal charm about him. . . . His appearance was rather repellent; his manners were coarse; his general attitude toward other people was rude, provocative, and cynical."

Stalin's writings at this time show him to have become increasingly disillusioned with those thinkers of the party who sat theorizing in cafés in the far-off capitals of Europe. He felt that the way to revive the movement was to have the workers take control of the party.

Now in his 30s, without friends or family, cut off from his political associates, it would not have been surprising had Stalin given up. But his patience was rewarded. Unexpected events would send Stalin on the path to ultimate power.

Tsarist soldiers stand guard over an imprisoned dissident at a labor camp in Siberia during the early 20th century. Siberia constituted a place of exile for opponents of the tsarist regime throughout Russia's pre-Revolutionary period.

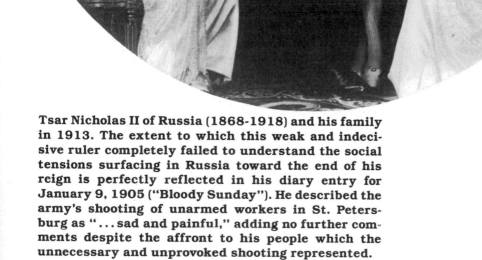

Tsar Nicholas II of Russia (1868-1918) and his family
in 1913. The extent to which this weak and indeci-
sive ruler completely failed to understand the social
tensions surfacing in Russia toward the end of his
reign is perfectly reflected in his diary entry for
January 9, 1905 ("Bloody Sunday"). He described the
army's shooting of unarmed workers in St. Petersburg as "...sad and painful," adding no further com-
ments despite the affront to his people which the
unnecessary and unprovoked shooting represented.

2

"A Gray Blur"

World War I broke out in Europe in 1914. It was a catastrophe for the Russian Empire, which mobilized over 15 million men for battle, but sent them to the front with hopelessly inadequate arms and equipment. Russia suffered greater casualties than any of the other warring nations. Food shortages developed in the cities. By the beginning of 1917 Russia was a war-weary nation.

In March riots broke out in the capital, which had been renamed Petrograd. The unrest rapidly spread to the tsar's guards, who refused to fire on the protestors. Within days the tsar abdicated and a provisional government made up of members of the Duma took control of the country.

Simultaneously, a competing source of power arose. This was the Petrograd Soviet of Workers' and Soldiers' Deputies. The Petrograd soviet's members were elected in factories and barracks of the military. Later, smaller soviets arose in other cities and towns and the countryside.

The main problem facing the provisional government was the war. Unwisely, its leaders decided to continue the war effort, and called for a large new offensive in July.

John Reed (1887-1920), the left-wing American journalist and author of _Ten Days That Shook The World_, his eyewitness account of events in Petrograd during the Russian Revolution in 1917. A Harvard-educated socialist, Reed helped organize a textile workers' strike in New Jersey in 1913.

Joseph Stalin around 1910. Stalin's activities throughout 1909 are poorly documented, and while several police reports (possibly forged, according to some experts) declare that Stalin continued his revolutionary activities in Baku and Tiflis, many Georgian subversives have since claimed that he temporarily abandoned his political involvements. Some historians consider such discrepancies evidence that Stalin was a police informer at around that time.

Alexander Kerensky, the Russian Social Democrat who became justice minister in the provisional government established after the revolution of February 1917. Overthrown in November 1917 by the Bolsheviks, who considered him insufficiently radical, Kerensky fled Petrograd for Paris where he pursued a career in journalism.

Meanwhile, a general political amnesty was declared. This action freed Stalin from exile, and he hurried to the capital. As the senior member of the central committee on the scene, he was the leader of the Bolsheviks.

His main problem was to decide what line should be taken toward the provisional government. Taking over the editorship of *Pravda,* he declared that the Bolsheviks would support the provisional government "insofar as it fights reaction or counterrevolution." Soon after, he became a member of the executive committee of the Petrograd soviet. A majority of the Petrograd soviet were Mensheviks, and Stalin carefully walked a narrow line between support for the Petrograd soviet and support for the provisional government. He explained the Bolshevik program in moderate slogans such as "land for the peasants, protection of labor for the workers, and the democratic republic for all citizens of Russia."

Stalin worked tirelessly to build up Bolshevik support. He met with shop stewards, agitators, and members of the soviet, advising them of the decisions of the central committee. Despite his abrasive personality, Stalin could be persuasive when he chose, especially with working people.

Bolshevik moderation ended when Lenin arrived from Switzerland on April 16. He unequivocally condemned the provisional government and its policies. He called for "all power to the soviets" and for an immediate withdrawal from the war.

Lenin needed all of his formidable powers of persuasion to get his followers to go along with this sudden change in policy. One of the earliest converts was Stalin, who easily shucked off the moderate attitude he had earlier advocated.

In July Trotsky declared his support for the Bolsheviks and Lenin. He brought with him his own followers and the skills in oratory and organization that he had shown in the 1905 revolution. The July riots protesting the government-backed offensive were organized in part by the Bolsheviks. As a result, the provisional government called for the arrest of their leaders. Trotsky was jailed, but Lenin escaped to Finland. Stalin again became the leading Bolshevik in Petrograd.

September was a crucial month for the Bolsheviks. The commander-in-chief of the Russian army, General L.G. Kornilov, was reported to be marching toward Petrograd to replace the new government. In a panic, the government released Trotsky and armed the soviet, hoping to use its members in the defense of the city.

The Kornilov threat did not succeed, but the damage was done. The Bolsheviks became a majority in the Petrograd soviet. Now the rallying cry "All power to the Soviets" became a call for Bolshevik revolution.

Stalin worked behind the scenes, acting as the liaison between the party central committee and the Petrograd soviet. A participant in the events later wrote of Stalin: "[He] gave me the impression . . . of a gray blur which flickered obscurely and left no trace." Stalin's ability to work unnoticed by others became one of his great strengths.

In any case, Stalin worked with Lenin and Trotsky in planning to take power by coup in November. The actual seizure of power, during the early morning hours of November 7, went smoothly. Soldiers and workers loyal to the Bolsheviks occupied strategic buildings. By the end of the day, the Winter Palace, headquarters of the provisional government, was taken. The Bolshevik Revolution, one of the most important events of the 20th century, was accomplished with little resistance or bloodshed.

The ruling body was called the Council of People's Commissars. For the first time, the party became known as the Communist Party. Trotsky was named commissar for foreign affairs, and Stalin was given the post of commissar for nationalities—that is, non-Russians in enclaves within the country.

Lenin found it difficult to carry out the policy of withdrawal from the war. Russia's chief enemy was Germany, the homeland of Marx. It was thought that the successful revolution in Russia would trigger a similar uprising in Germany. When this did not come about, Lenin called for an immediate

Tsar Nicholas II of Russia and his wife, the Tsarina Alexandra, in 1904. Alexandra had emerged as the dominant partner in the relationship soon after their marriage in 1894. She displayed a protectiveness toward her husband which, combined with her political and social ineptitude, severely damaged the prestige of the Romanov royal dynasty in the eyes of Russians of all social classes.

Russian troops rest prior to taking part in the Battle of Tannenberg (August 26—31, 1914). The Russian military effort absorbed almost 15 million men during the course of World War I, devastating the country's agriculture and industry and thus creating shortages of food and goods which greatly increased social unrest.

Russian soldiers loyal to the revolutionary cause patrol the streets of Petrograd in April 1917. Stalin's original intention to cooperate with the provisional government received immediate modification that same month when Lenin returned from exile. Lenin declared for the workers' soviets, condemning the provisional government as a bourgeois institution which did not serve the workers' interests.

peace with no annexations.

The Germans, aware of Russia's military weakness, did not agree to Lenin's proposal. They wanted a large chunk of Russian territory.

Lenin was willing to make peace at any price. He agreed to the Treaty of Brest-Litovsk, which lost for Russia most of the Ukraine, Poland, and the small states along the Baltic Sea. No other decision of Lenin's aroused so much opposition. Stalin was one of the few top Bolsheviks who supported Lenin. The other socialist parties, which had been included in the government formed after the November revolution, withdrew in protest. From that time on, the Soviet Union was ruled by a one-party government.

The Bolsheviks faced opposition of a more serious kind. The former head of the provisional government escaped from Petrograd and began to organize military units to oppose the Bolsheviks. Civil war between the "White" Russians and Lenin's "Red" Russians would drag on for three years. Lenin moved the government to Moscow, which he believed to be a safer location.

Revolution in Russia did not quite fit the theories of Marx. Marx thought that revolution would

An official Soviet sketch of Molotov, Stalin, and Lenin working in the offices of *Pravda* ("Truth"), the Bolshevik newspaper, prior to the Russian Revolution. Stalin's self-promoting 1951 claim that he had founded the newspaper was a gross exaggeration. Lenin's personal account of the birth of *Pravda* names Stalin as but one of 20 contributors to the journal.

occur in an industrialized society where the proletariat formed a majority of the population. But Russia was a backward country where the majority of people were peasant farmers.

Lenin encouraged the peasants to seize the land and property of their landlords. But granting individual private property was not Lenin's real goal. He sought to reorganize the economy by having the government take over factories, banks, and foreign trade.

This phase of the Bolshevik regime is known as "war communism." In order to feed the Red Army and the populations in the cities, the government requisitioned food from the peasants. Violent means

Leon Trotsky in 1918, sporting his customary leather campaign jacket.

The cruiser *Aurora* lies at anchor before the Winter Palace in Petrograd, November 6, 1917. Trotsky and his colleagues had secured the loyalty of the *Aurora's* crew that same day, ordering them to disregard all instructions from the provisional government.

sometimes had to be used in the collection of food. Workers were uprooted from their homes and sent wherever they were needed. To many ordinary people, war communism seemed as harsh as the tsar's rule.

The White Russians gained support. Russia's former allies, alarmed by the prospect of a Bolshevik Russia, sent troops in 1918 to help overthrow the Lenin government.

Stalin's most significant mission in the civil war was to help organize the defense of the city of Tsaritsyn on the Volga River. This was a key city because it was near the greatest food-growing region. Stalin was to arrange for food shipments to Moscow.

In July 1918 he reported to Lenin that profiteering and chaos were widespread. He ordered rationing and price controls. He also criticized Trotsky, now

Bolshevik troops in Petrograd assault the Winter Palace, seat of the provisional government, on November 7, 1917. Moderate socialists in Petrograd, aghast at the Bolshevik coup, realized immediately that their influence had received a blow from which it was never to recover.

Soviet and German delegates negotiate the Treaty of Brest-Litovsk in March 1918. The typically aristocratic German diplomats detested having to deal with the representatives of revolutionary Russia, some of whom taunted their German counterparts by blowing cigarette smoke directly into their faces across the conference table and handing out communist propaganda to the soldiers who had escorted them to the conference.

Major General F.C. Poole, a senior officer with the British interventionary forces in the Soviet Union, poses with anti-Bolshevik cavalrymen in Murmansk in 1918. Allied efforts to undermine the Bolshevik government proved ineffective and served to increase the support of the Russian people for their new communist rulers.

minister of war, for his choice of commanders in the area.

Trotsky succeeded in persuading Lenin to recall Stalin later in the fall. By this time the White forces in the area had been overcome. Rather than make Stalin's recall seem a reprimand, as Trotsky wished, Lenin sent a special train for him. He returned to Moscow with ceremonies befitting a conquering hero. Some years later, the name of Tsaritsyn was changed to Stalingrad.

Stalin believed he was a great military leader. Decorations were given to those who had performed outstanding acts of bravery. One of Stalin's allies proposed his name for the Order of the Red Banner.

Members of the Petrograd Soviet of Workers' and Soldiers' Deputies parade in 1919, the year which saw the first meeting of the Comintern (Communist International) in Moscow. Lenin and Trotsky used the conference, organized to promote and coordinate revolutionary efforts abroad, to appeal to workers throughout the world, asking them to pressure their governments to cease from armed intervention against the Soviet state.

A less admiring comrade remarked, "Stalin can't live unless he has what someone else has."

For the rest of the civil war, Stalin acted as a trouble-shooter in various places. His reports frequently contained barbs at Trotsky. They were ineffectual, for Trotsky earned glory and respect for his brilliant organization of the Red Army. Trotsky's work was crucial to the eventual victory of the Reds, but the long-term effects of Stalin's jealousy would prove fatal.

By 1920 most of the White forces were in retreat and most of the foreign troops withdrawn from the country. The next year Lenin inaugurated the New Economic Policy (NEP) which relaxed some of the controls of war communism. The major industries were to be owned by the state as part of the "socialist sector." Some private trade and small, privately-owned industry were permitted. Farming remained in the hands of individuals.

The NEP was opposed by some Bolsheviks as a concession to the capitalist system. Stalin, as ever, was loyal to his mentor. He said, "Russia is now undergoing an outburst of the forces of production of the kind experienced by the United States after the Civil War." And in fact, the economy did improve, aided by bountiful harvests.

As commissar of nationalities, Stalin had to decide how to deal with the national independence movements that had grown in tsarist Russia. He announced the independence of Finland. Soon, however, national leaders in the Ukraine, Baltic Sea area, Caucasus, Siberia, and Central Asia demanded independence as well. These areas were important to the economic health of Soviet Russia. Stalin decreed the new principle that self-determination should be the privilege of the working masses and not the bourgeoisie.

Nevertheless, Stalin's native Georgia was recognized as a separate republic in 1918. It had a government controlled by Mensheviks, most of whom were old comrades of Stalin's.

Stalin convinced Lenin that the Georgian Mensheviks were abusing the rights of Bolsheviks. Lenin agreed to Stalin's proposal for organizing a Bolshevik coup in Georgia.

Stalin showed what uses he could make of military power. The Red Army installed a pro-Bolshevik government in Georgia. In effect, Georgia resumed its old place as part of a Russian empire—now a Soviet empire. But under Stalin's orders, all opposition was suppressed in the most brutal fashion. Even the Georgian Communist Party was purged of dissident elements—an action that was to be repeated on a greater scale in Russia in the 1930s.

Lenin was alarmed by the reports of Stalin's actions in Georgia. Before he could take action, however, he suffered a stroke in 1922. While he was recovering, Stalin telephoned Lenin's wife, who served as his secretary and confidante. Stalin apparently believed she was turning Lenin against him, and he berated and threatened her.

When Lenin recovered, he sent a cold and angry letter to Stalin, demanding an apology. Relations between the two men were never again the same. However, Lenin suffered another stroke and was not able to resume his leadership. He died on January 21, 1924.

The death of the revolution's leader was the occasion of widespread sorrow. It was decided to embalm his body and display it permanently as a shrine. The anniversary of his death was declared a day of national mourning. Petrograd was renamed Leningrad. The other Bolshevik leaders, aware that their popularity did not match Lenin's, began what

Every honest Communist will fight against bourgeois society to his last breath, in word and in deed and if necessary with arms in hand. The propaganda of the Communist International will be pernicious for you, the imperialists. It is the historical mission of the Communist International to be the gravedigger of bourgeois society.
—from the text of a resolution adopted in 1922 by the Communist International

Joseph Stalin and Kliment Voroshilov in Tsaritsyn in 1918. Voroshilov, appointed to command the Red Army units on the Tsaritsyn front on July 10, 1918, became a member of the central committee of the Communist Party in 1921 and went on to play a great part in modernizing the Soviet forces during the 1920s and 1930s.

was almost a religious cult in his honor. The teachings of Lenin became as important as those of Marx.

The question of a successor to Lenin now arose. Lenin's power came not from the party and government posts he held, but from the force of his personality. His ability to convince others of the rightness of his views made him the undisputed leader. With his death there was no one with the same qualities.

Stalin had used his own posts wisely. As commissar of nationalities he had dealt directly with the affairs of nearly half the nation. About 65 million of the total population of 140 million were non-Russians. He could count on the support of Bolsheviks in non-Russian areas.

In 1922 Lenin had appointed Stalin general sec-

Soviet schoolchildren in Moscow prepare to join a parade celebrating the second anniversary of the Russian Revolution. Free public education, which was a major element of Bolshevik proposals for social reform in 1917, fast became a reality following the end of the civil war in 1920, and increased literacy throughout the Soviet Union to levels undreamed of in the tsarist era.

The wooden tomb in Moscow which housed Lenin's body from 1926 until 1930, when the Soviet government authorized construction of the massive granite and porphyry mausoleum which stands to this day. Here, until 1961, Stalin's body rested beside Lenin's remains.

Female members of the Red Army undergo drill instruction during the savage civil war which afflicted the Soviet Union between 1917 and 1920.

retary of the party. This seemingly innocuous post gave him responsibility for party appointments, promotions, and demotions. Many medium-level officials owed their loyalty to the man who had appointed them.

Stalin also belonged to the five-member politburo, which guided the political affairs of the central committee. A complicated bureaucracy had already established itself in control of the country. And Stalin was a master of detail of this kind, a patient plodder who knew how to use the levers of power.

However, there was a surprise in store for Stalin. At the meeting of the central committee four months

Lev Kamenev (1883-1936) with his wife in 1930. Appointed vice-president of the Soviet Union in 1923, Kamenev went on to hold several additional high positions in the Soviet government despite the fact that many of his colleagues considered him a Trotskyite and therefore suspect.

after Lenin's death, Lenin's "last testament" was read. He had dictated it when the memory of Stalin's insult to his wife was still fresh. In it he suggested that Stalin be relieved from his post as general secretary because "Stalin is too coarse and this fault, though quite tolerable in relations among us communists, becomes intolerable in the office of general secretary."

Stalin was publicly humiliated by the man who had been his hero and mentor. He would regard it as a betrayal by the one man whom he had always supported and respected. The lesson that Stalin drew was never to trust anyone.

An eyewitness to the meeting where the "testament" was read wrote, "Terrible embarrassment paralyzed all those present. Stalin sitting on the steps of the rostrum looked small and miserable. I studied him closely. In spite of his self-control and show of calm, it was obvious that his fate was at stake."

But Gregori Zinoviev, another member of the politburo with his own ambitions to replace Lenin, spoke in Stalin's behalf. He pointed out Stalin's "harmonious cooperation" in the months since Lenin's death. Another high official, Lev Kamenev, proposed that Stalin be allowed to keep his post, and that Lenin's will not be disclosed at the forthcoming party congress. Trotsky, whom everyone knew to be Stalin's enemy, remained silent. Over the protest of Lenin's widow, it was decided to allow Stalin to keep his post and read Lenin's will to only a few selected delegates to the congress.

Zinoviev and Kamenev had saved Stalin not out of friendship or respect. They anticipated a struggle with Trotsky for leadership of the party, and saw in Stalin a likely ally. They made the great mistake of many of Stalin's opponents—they underestimated his abilities.

Joseph Stalin converses with Lenin in 1922. Stalin greatly prized this photograph and often contended that his previous close association with the architect of the Soviet state justified his political supremacy.

Mikhail Kalinin (1875-1946), president of the Soviet Union from 1923 until his death, inspects livestock on a collective farm in 1929.

A Bolshevik electioneer campaigns among the peasants in a rural district of the Soviet Union in 1928, the year in which the Soviet government issued an instruction entitled *On Penal Policy and the Regime of Places of Confinement*, openly stating its intention to deal severely with dissidents and criminals.

Most of the inner circle of the party were intellectuals and Marxist scholars. Stalin usually sat in silence while the others debated the finer points of Marxist economics. Despite Trotsky's appraisal of him as "our party's most eminent mediocrity," he had an uncanny ability to spot weaknesses in others. And he had the ability to work long hours, tirelessly going over the details of day-to-day party work.

So it was that Stalin remained in his post of party secretary, biding his time while his allies Zinoviev and Kamenev went after Trotsky. Their weapons were chiefly words. They criticized Trotsky for such things as his policy of attempting large industrial projects in too short a time. Being wrong

Soviet peasants arrive in Moscow in 1922, seeking relief from the famine which afflicted many parts of the country between 1921 and 1922. Lenin's New Economic Policy of 1921 (which Stalin strongly supported) boosted the economy out of the stagnation which had contributed to the famine, and briefly created something resembling a free market within the Soviet Union.

Kliment Voroshilov, Joseph Stalin, and President Kalinin attend a party meeting in 1932. At that time the government's relentless collectivization of Soviet agriculture had created famines throughout the country's grain-growing regions more terrible than those which severely affected the nation throughout the early 1920s.

about economic matters was a serious fault among the followers of Marx.

Trotsky found himself with few allies. His arrogance had offended others besides Stalin, and in votes of the central committee he was frequently the loser. He was also hampered by his belief that the party could not be wrong because, as he said, the party was the instrument of history. "One can be right," said Trotsky, "only with the party and through the party, since history has created no other paths to the realization of what is right."

The party decreed in 1925 that Trotsky be removed from his post as commissar of war, and he accepted the decision. In the same way, Stalin was able to use loyalty to the party in the 1930s to dispose of his real and imagined enemies without serious opposition.

With Trotsky out of the way, Stalin now allied himself with Nikolai Bukharin, the leading Marxist theoretician following Lenin's death. Bukharin began to argue against the policies of Zinoviev and Kamenev, and as Trotsky had before them, they became isolated within the party councils.

Many of these intra-party arguments during the 1920s were about government policy toward the farmers of Russia. Lenin, as we have seen, permitted the private ownership of land. Zinoviev and Kamenev wanted to follow a policy of forced "collectivization." That is, the farmland would be taken over by the state and the peasants be assigned to work on large farms, just as the industrial workers were assigned jobs in factories.

Bukharin argued that Lenin's New Economic Policy was correct. The party agreed, and Kamenev and Zinoviev lost their former influence.

All this time, as one observer said, Stalin contributed not one idea to the discussion. The others found no fault in this. As one old Marxist once said to him in a meeting, "Now, stop that, Koba, you are making yourself ridiculous. Everybody knows that theory is not your field."

What Stalin was doing was continuing to appoint his own followers to the ranks of party leaders. The theoreticians such as Zinoviev, Kamenev, and Bukharin were content to leave the petty day-to-day details to Stalin. He merely carried out the plans they had decided on.

Stalin seemed quite moderate and conciliatory. In 1925 when Zinoviev and Kamenev were demanding the expulsion of Trotsky from the party, he said, "The policy of cutting off heads is fraught with major dangers for the party . . . today you cut off one head, tomorrow a second, and then a third: who would remain in the party?"

By 1928 Stalin was ready to act on his own. He announced a new agricultural policy in opposition to Bukharin's views. The central committee voted in Stalin's favor. The party had spoken; Bukharin was expelled from his important posts.

Thus it was that when Stalin celebrated his 50th birthday in 1929, he had no rivals for power. Trotsky had by this time not only been expelled from the party, but from the Soviet Union itself. In the decade that followed, Stalin would have a free hand in carrying out his own plans. And his true nature would be unleashed at last.

> *There [in Petrograd] among Russian workers—the liberators of oppressed peoples and the pioneers of the proletarian struggle of all countries and all peoples—I received my third baptism in the revolutionary fire. There, in Russia, under Lenin's guidance, I became a master worker of revolution.*
> —JOSEPH STALIN
> writing in 1926 of his part in the Russian Revolution

A 1918 Soviet poster commemorating the Russian Revolution of 1917.

3
The Gods Are Athirst

Now firmly in control of the Soviet Union, Stalin began to apply his own methods to changing the country. The Soviet economy was still concentrated in agriculture. By the mid-1920s there were about 25 million farms in the Soviet Union. Many produced only enough to feed the families who worked them.

The more successful farmers, called *kulaks*, gradually increased their production. But they were reluctant to sell their products at the low prices offered by the state, which had the responsibility of feeding the cities and their industrial workers. From a purely practical standpoint, far too much manpower was taken up by farming.

In 1928 Stalin announced the first Five Year Plan. It seemed a modest proposal to gradually collectivize the farms—bring them under state control—through persuasion and voluntary action. It was felt that once the peasants saw the benefits of modern agriculture, they would join the state-run collective farms.

The peasants, and especially the kulaks, were more stubborn than Stalin expected. Stalin then turned to the policy of divide-and-conquer which had served him so well in his rise to power. He

If we ruled only by fear, not a man would have stood by us. The working classes would have destroyed any power that attempted to rule by fear.
—JOSEPH STALIN
during an interview with German author Emil Ludwig in 1931

Leon Trotsky in 1927, shortly before Stalin exiled him to Alma-Ata in Siberia as a prelude to his expulsion from the Soviet Union in 1929. In conducting his gradual erosion of Trotsky's power and influence, Stalin cleverly concentrated on destroying the support which Trotsky had previously enjoyed among Soviet intellectuals and Red Army officers.

Joseph Stalin meets with smiling Soviet peasants while visiting a collective farm in 1935, two years after he had established a nationwide manpower policy which effectively confined the peasants to their farms. Similar policies concerning industrial workers, enacted in 1939, further contributed to the inflexibility of the Soviet "managed economy" and reflected Stalin's obsession with social uniformity.

Soviet peasants at work in their fields in 1924. Four years later Stalin announced the inception of the first Five Year Plan and set about changing the face of Soviet agriculture forever. In January 1930 the Soviet government stepped up its war on private farmers, approving a resolution entitled *On Measures to Eliminate Kulak Households in Districts of Total Collectivization.*

declared a "class war" on the kulaks, offering the poorer peasants the kulaks' livestock, tools, and machinery. The kulaks' land would be absorbed by the collective farms.

To enforce his policy of eliminating the kulaks as a class, Stalin sent to the countryside industrial workers, party leaders, army units, and the secret police. The war against the kulaks turned into a war on the peasants. Villages that resisted "voluntary" association were surrounded by army units and forced to surrender. Resisting villages were destroyed, their inhabitants killed or deported. Millions were sent to Siberia and the Arctic regions.

These harsh measures had their effect. In 1928 only 1.7% of the peasants were on collective farms. The figure rose to 4.1% in October 1929, and then jumped to 21% in January 1930. By March, 1930, an astonishing 58% of the peasant families were living on collective farms.

Joseph Stalin meets with construction workers on the site of a new power station in 1933. The ideological frenzy which accompanied Soviet industrialization under the terms of the first Five Year Plan often led to great inefficiency and lack of coordination. Many new structures, erected against impossible deadlines, collapsed before they were completed.

This success had its cost, and not only in the lives of peasants killed or deported. In a show of bitter resistance, the peasants destroyed their livestock and tools and burned their crops or let them rot in the fields. Between 1929 and 1934 the number of cattle in the country dropped from 58 million to 33.5 million. The number of horses dropped from 32.6 million to 17.3 million. Even greater losses occurred among hogs, sheep, and goats. Livestock totals did not reach their pre-Five Year Plan levels again until the mid-1950s.

Stalin reacted to this stunning failure by putting the blame on others. In a 1930 article in *Pravda* titled "Dizzy with Success," he blamed the turmoil on overzealous party workers. They had not fully understood his directives and became "dizzy with the success" of their work. Posing as the defender of the peasants, Stalin said "collective farms cannot be set up by force," and to do so would be "stupid and reactionary."

The Dnieprostroy Dam on the Dnieper River constituted one of the greatest achievements of Stalinist industrial planning. During World War II, in accordance with the "scorched earth" policy whereby the Soviets destroyed their crops and relocated their light industry rather than have it fall into German hands intact, the dam was destroyed in order to deny the Germans access to electrical power in the region.

Joseph Stalin meets with delegates to a party congress in 1930. By this time Stalin's expulsion of Leon Trotsky from the Soviet Union in 1929 had further consolidated his political supremacy and enabled him to pursue his harsh policies without interference from Trotsky's former supporters.

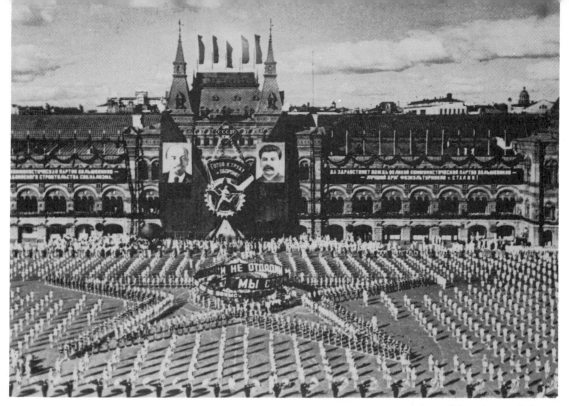

After that, the drive toward collectivization slowed but did not stop. By 1938 there were 242,400 collective farms containing 93.4% of the peasant families.

This numerical success was accompanied by widespread famine. No one really knows the total of people who starved to death. As for the kulaks, official sources put the number killed or deported at five million. But the number may have been higher.

The first Five Year Plan also set new goals for industry. In the party debates of the 1920s Stalin had called Trotsky, Zinoviev, and Kamenev "super-industrializers" when they called for an industrial growth rate of 20% a year. But by the second year of the Five Year Plan, Stalin was calling for a growth rate of 50%.

Earlier, Stalin had laughed at plans to build a hydroelectric dam on the Dnieper River, comparing it to a peasant buying a gramophone instead of a cow. The dam was the first major accomplishment of the Five Year Plan.

Portraits of Lenin and Stalin dominate the proceedings at a Moscow sports parade during the 1930s. The spectacular abilities of Soviet athletes did not become fully apparent to the Western nations until after Stalin's death, when his successors reversed the dictator's policy of not allowing Soviet teams to compete at events in "capitalist countries."

Vyacheslav Molotov, the Soviet statesman who achieved great prominence during the Stalin era. Appointed commissar for foreign affairs in 1939, Molotov was the chief architect of the Soviet-German non-aggression treaty signed in Moscow in August 1939.

Stalin's views had changed because he now saw the need for developing heavy industry in the country. The success of the collective farms depended on the use of modern agricultural machinery—which could only be produced by a highly industrialized country.

Stalin felt he could accomplish the goals of the plan through organization and encouragement. The party assumed close control over every sector of the economy. All important industrial decisions were made by the party.

Workers were praised for their efforts in the campaign to "build socialism." Progress boards displayed in factories compared goals with actual output. Workers who fell behind were publicly criticized. Laborers could be cited as "Heroes of the Soviet Union." A miner named Stakhanov became famous for greatly surpassing his personal quota (by 1300%!) Outstanding workers became known as "Stakhanovites."

At the same time, the workers were asked to accept the lower wages and shortages of food which had resulted from collectivization. Many workers became disgruntled and absenteeism increased.

Stalin's response was greater repression. In 1932 an internal passport system was instituted. Everyone had to carry national identity papers and was required to stay in that part of the country where his or her assigned job was.

Nadezhda Alliluyeva, the wife of Joseph Stalin, with their daughter Svetlana in 1930. After Nadezhda's suicide in 1932 Stalin often visited her grave. The sincerity of his grief can be gauged not only from the regularity of such visits but also from the fact that he commissioned a white marble column supporting an effigy of Nadezhda to be erected over the grave.

Joseph Stalin with his daughter Svetlana in 1937. The name Svetlana derives from the word *svet,* which in Russian means "radiance" or "daylight."

Sergei Mironovich Kirov (1888-1934), the Leningrad party leader and loyal associate of Stalin whose assassination in 1934 provided the dictator with a perfect excuse for instituting the massive purges which terrorized Soviet society until 1938. Following Kirov's death, Stalin drastically increased security measures in the Kremlin to the point where visitors to his office underwent four interrogations and searches before arriving in his presence.

Stalin was ever concerned about the threat from the capitalist nations. Replying to criticism of the excessive pace of the industrialization, he said, "To reduce the tempo would mean to fall behind. And those who fall behind get beaten. But we do not want to be beaten. No, we refuse to be beaten. One feature . . . of old Russia was the continual beating she suffered because of her backwardness. . . . We are fifty or a hundred years behind the advanced countries. We must make good this distance in ten years. Either we do it, or we shall be crushed."

Nevertheless, the speed and unrealistic goals of the Five Year Plan led to mistakes and waste. As always, Stalin could not admit a mistake. He found the term "wreckers" useful in accounting for failures. Wreckers in the system were promoting famine, sabotaging production of coal and iron, causing shortages in the production of electric power, and so on. Wreckers were to be found in all stages of production, from workers to managers.

Because the real goal of the Five Year Plan was to make the Soviet Union a modern nation, it carried over into all areas of Soviet life. Schools were established to train workers in new skills. A campaign

Gregori Zinoviev (1883-1936), the prominent Soviet politician who in 1936 confessed his involvement in a conspiracy to overthrow Joseph Stalin.

to reduce illiteracy began. Railway lines and highways were built to improve the country's primitive transportation system. New factories were built in the Ural Mountain region and farther east, to put them in locations defensible in the event of war.

In spite of the ghastly methods he used, Stalin's industrialization and collectivization programs began to get results. Two more Five Year Plans followed the first, and toward the end of the 1930s Russia's industrial power was catching up with Germany's. The standard of living of the average person was still very much lower than in other developed countries, but Russia's output of coal, oil, steel, and electricity was rising. The collective farms began to benefit from new machinery and methods and produced enough to prevent major famines.

The national tensions brought on by the Five Year Plan coincided with a crisis in Stalin's personal life. In 1919 he had married for the second time. His wife was Nadezhda Alliluyeva, the daughter of an old comrade of his. They lived in a modest apartment in the Kremlin. She was much younger than he was, and known as a beautiful woman.

Nadezhda moved freely about Moscow, talking to students and workers. She heard tales of the brutal repression in the countryside and pleaded with Stalin to ease his methods. His refusal put a strain on their relationship. She could not reconcile her own revolutionary ideals with what her husband was doing.

At a party in 1932 celebrating the anniversary of the revolution, Stalin was in a drunken mood. He spoke rudely to his wife in front of others. She rushed out of the room and later that night committed suicide. She left a note reproaching Stalin for his personal and political failings.

Their daughter Svetlana has said, "My mother's death was a dreadful crushing blow, and it destroyed his faith in friends and people in general." Stalin moved to a different apartment in the Kremlin and never again visited the summer house they had shared. He built a new house at Kuntsevo where he lived alone for the next 20 years when he was not in the Kremlin.

But he never forgot her. Enlarged photographs of her in happy poses were in both his apartment and country house. He talked obsessively about her, wondering why his "closest and most faithful friend" would "betray" him.

For a short time, Nadezhda's death seems to have affected his emotional balance. At one meeting of the politburo he offered his resignation. The scene was similar to the one at which Lenin's testament was read. Finally one of the members, Vyacheslav Molotov, jumped up and shouted, "Stop it! Stop it!

We are convinced that the foreign capitalists, who will be obliged to work on the terms we offer them, will dig their own grave.... With every additional shovel of coal, with every additional load of oil that we in Russia obtain through the help of foreign technique, capital will be digging its own grave.
—LEV KAMENEV
politburo member, shortly before the signing of the Anglo-Soviet Trade Agreement in 1921

Joseph Stalin and other high-ranking Soviet officials carry the urn containing the ashes of slain Leningrad party leader Sergei Kirov at his funeral in Moscow in 1934. Kirov's murder convinced Stalin of the existence of a widespread conspiracy against the Soviet government.

Soviet troops parade in Moscow's Red Square during the May Day celebrations in 1931. Although the Red Army underwent modernization during the 1930s, Stalin's purge of 35,000 of its best officers after 1937 severely affected its fighting ability.

You have the party's confidence!" Molotov was one of the few high party officials who would escape the purge trials of the 1930s.

Stalin's personal characteristics often made others uneasy. Even Lenin finally turned against him because of "coarse" behavior. Stalin also nurtured a suspiciousness of enemies, a growing fear of betrayal, a feeling that he could trust no one. In the last half of the 1930s these aspects of his personality developed into a paranoid madness that devoured anyone who could conceivably be thought of as threatening to him. This was the period of the great purge.

It began at the end of 1934, when the party leader of Leningrad, Sergei Kirov, was assassinated. The assassin, a student, was said to be part of a group that was planning the deaths of Stalin and other party leaders. Thousands of people were arrested in Leningrad as suspected members of the group.

Zinoviev and Kamenev were among those accused of involvement in the plot. Zinoviev was sentenced to ten years of forced labor, and Kamenev five years. Thousands of others were deported to Siberia.

That was only the beginning. Lenin had begun a secret police organization to guard against capitalist plotters, but under Stalin the secret police greatly increased in power and scope. A special committee headed by Stalin was formed to "liquidate the enemies of the people." Loyal party members were urged to help find the hidden enemies. Many responded with denunciations of their comrades.

The first purge trial was held in secret, but the "show trials" that followed, in 1936, 1937, and 1938, were carefully orchestrated public spectacles.

Surprisingly, many of the accused admitted their guilt. Zinoviev and Kamenev were brought back for the 1936 show trial. Both admitted being part of a conspiracy to overthrow Stalin and the government. Kamenev named others who were part of the conspiracy. The prosecutor summed up the case with the words, "I demand that all these mad dogs be shot." The court agreed.

Arrests spread beyond party members to anyone with any record of opposition to any government policy. Ordinary workers, peasants, anyone who had secretly visited a foreign country were caught up in the ever-widening net. People lived in constant fear that any conversation might bring the

Soviet judges preside at a Moscow "show trial" in 1936. So savagely did the courts act against alleged enemies of the people that in 1939 Stalin reported that party membership had "dropped" from 1,874,888 in 1934 to 1,588,852 in 1939! Stalin's paranoia had resulted in the murder of almost 300,000 members of the organization which represented his main power base within Soviet society.

secret police in the middle of the night. Even remarks made in conversations long ago could bring on the fearful midnight knock, for Stalin apparently never forgot a slight. People who had inadvertently "insulted" him years earlier now found themselves victims of his deadly wrath.

The sheer numbers of those arrested, which ran into the millions, alarmed and confused people. It was thought that there must really be a conspiracy, for not all of these charges could possibly be false. And besides, so many of the accused made confessions.

The investigators, the secret police, grew adept at forcing confessions. An investigation sometimes included physical torture. Questioning could go on as long as a suspect protested innocence. Threats against a suspect's family members were made. Under these conditions, it was hardly surprising that so many confessed.

During the trials Stalin was nowhere to be seen. The purported victim of all these crimes was usually in his summer home on the Black Sea. The head of the secret police, Nikolai Yezhov, was widely believed to be behind the madness. The period is remembered as the Yezhovshchina.

Ordinary people really did not believe Stalin was personally involved. Many who realized the injustice of the purge remarked, "If only Stalin knew!" This attitude was found even among the victims. One party member who survived his prison sentence wrote, "When they arrested me . . . I felt such horror, not for myself but for the party. I couldn't understand why they were arresting old Bolsheviks. For what? . . . . I told myself something horrible was happening in the party, probably wrecking. . . . Not for one minute, though I spent two and a half years in prison . . . did I ever accuse Stalin. I always stood up for Stalin when other prisoners cursed him. I would say: 'No, it cannot be that Stalin has permitted all that has happened. . . . It cannot be.' "

During the 1930s Stalin was interviewed by many people from the West. He was anxious to make a good impression, for he was seeking loans and

William C. Bullitt (1891-1967), the American diplomat who became the first United States ambassador to the Soviet Union in 1933. Bullitt later served as ambassador to France.

Nikolai Yezhov, the head of the Soviet secret police whose name became so closely associated with the Stalinist purges that the period of his murderous ascendancy is often remembered as the Yezhovshchina. Previous to his promotion in 1936, Yezhov had been a comparatively obscure member of Joseph Stalin's secretarial staff.

support from other nations. Lion Feuchtwanger, a writer, met Stalin and described him as "a simple, good-hearted man, who appreciated humor and was not offended by criticism of himself."

The Soviet press printed pictures of Stalin at collective farms with smiling peasants around him. He began to adopt the title of "Great Father of his people."

Some knew the truth. In 1936 Bukharin was allowed to make a trip to Paris. There, he was asked why Stalin's victims included so many of the old Bolsheviks who had made the revolution.

Bukharin summed up Stalin's motives: " He is unhappy at not being able to convince everyone, himself included, that he is greater than everyone;

Kamenev was shot first. He did not resist, offered no complaint. He left his cell in silence, and as if in a dream descended into the execution cellar. After the first revolver shot . . . he let out an "ah!" of stupefaction and fell down. He was still alive. Lieutenant Vasiukov . . . gave the dying man a kick with his boot. A second bullet in the head finished Kamenev.

—excerpt from reports in the foreign press regarding the execution of Lev Kamenev, Stalin's rival, in 1936. There is substantial evidence that the reports were leaked by Soviet secret police officers who attended the execution

Nikolai Krylenko (1885-1938), people's commissar for justice, addresses the court at a Moscow "show trial" in 1936. Krylenko had briefly commanded the Bolshevik armies during 1917 and 1918, promoted from the lowly rank of ensign by Lenin to replace General Dukhonin, who had questioned the Bolsheviks' authority to demand a ceasefire with Germany.

and this unhappiness of his may be . . . the only human trait in him. But what is not human, but rather something devilish, is that because of this unhappiness he cannot help taking revenge on people. . . . If someone speaks better than he does, that man is doomed! Stalin will not let him live, because that man is a perpetual reminder that he, Stalin, is not the first and best."

Yet Bukharin, after remarking to another friend in Paris, "And now he is going to kill me," returned to Stalin's Russia. He was shot in March 1938 after making a partial confession.

Because the party controlled all records, no one really knows the number of Stalin's victims. Estimates of those arrested in the purges range from 7 million to 23 million people. It is known that of the

> *Stalin was able to see the world only through the prism of his own ambitions and his own fears. The foreigner who talked to Stalin could never be sure just what he was dealing with—whether it was the interests of the movement or the interests of Stalin which stood in his path.*
> —GEORGE F. KENNAN
> American diplomat and historian

Lion Feuchtwanger (1884-1958), the German novelist and dramatist who interviewed Stalin in 1937. Feuchtwanger described the treason trial which he attended as "a debate conducted . . . by educated men who were trying to get at the truth." Such an impression of the trial demonstrates the efficiency with which the Stalin regime was capable of inflicting hardship on its own people while making the process look like material and moral progress to sympathetic foreign observers.

Leon Trotsky's office in Mexico City, where he was assassinated by an agent acting on Stalin's orders on August 21, 1940.

140 members of the central committee elected in 1934, only 15 still had their freedom in 1937. Officially, the central committee was the ruling body of the party.

The Soviet military forces also suffered. Perhaps two-thirds of all officers from the rank of colonel upward were liquidated. The loss of experienced officers was to have a disastrous effect on the army's ability to defend the nation.

After the 1938 trials, Stalin's thirst for blood apparently abated. He replaced Yezhov as head of the secret police with Lavrenti Beria. Not long after, Yezhov was arrested. Two years later, in the midst of a conversation, Stalin remarked, "Yezhov was a rat; in 1938 he killed many innocent people. We shot him for that!"

One of the most frequent accusations at the purge trials was the crime of being a "Trotskyite." Trotsky himself had escaped, and was living in Mexico by 1940. But he was not beyond Stalin's reach. A secret agent of Stalin's won his way into Trotsky's confidence and then crushed his skull with an axe. Trotsky was seated at his desk, and his blood spattered onto the manuscript of a biography of Stalin he was working on.

Stalin reigned supreme over a country drenched in blood. There was no possible opposition to him within the Soviet Union. All sectors of the economy were under his control. He had more power than any other ruler in history. But there were still more enemies to worry about. He would never be rid of them.

Leon Trotsky lies dead in a Mexico City hospital on August 22, 1940. Trotsky, whom the government prosecutors at the Moscow treason trials constantly invoked as the figurehead of anti-Soviet conspiracy, had outlived his usefulness to Stalin as an excuse for a reign of terror.

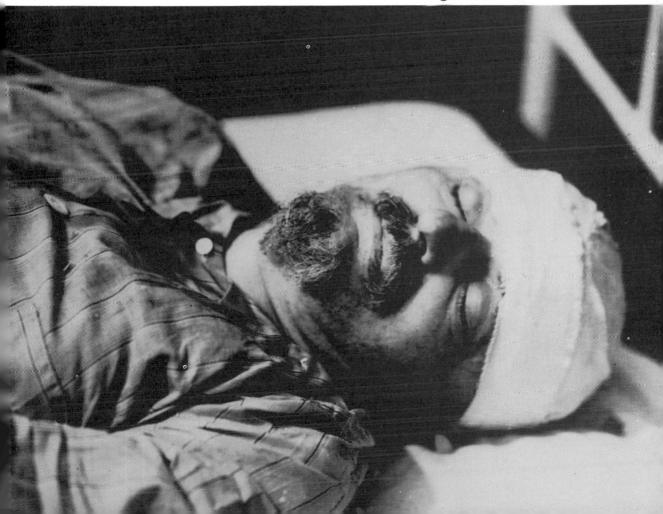

4

"For Country and for Stalin"

While Stalin annihilated millions of imaginary enemies at home, a real threat outside the country was growing ever stronger. In 1933 Adolf Hitler and his Nazi Party came to power in Germany. Hitler was an ardent foe of communism. He was also determined to rearm Germany and win back the land and power it had lost in World War I.

The threat of Hitler caused the Soviet Union to take a more active part in international affairs. It joined the League of Nations and advocated collective action to stop German aggression. Stalin signed mutual defense treaties with France and Czechoslovakia, opened diplomatic relations with the United States, and participated in the Spanish Civil War in opposition to the Nazi-backed Franco forces. For the first time, Stalin permitted communist parties in other countries to cooperate with noncommunist parties and governments.

Stalin watched with growing unease as Hitler built up Germany's military forces and reoccupied the formerly German Rhineland without serious opposition. Most disturbing of all was the Munich Pact, in which Britain and France persuaded Czechoslovakia to surrender part of its territory to

Soviet infantry parade during maneuvers on the Manchurian border in August 1938. In March 1939 Stalin made a speech in which he bitterly attacked the Western press for printing what he called lies concerning "the weakness of the Red Army" and "the lack of morale in the Red Air Force."

General Francisco Franco (1892-1975), the Spanish fascist leader. Stalin sent hundreds of Soviet military and political experts to fight against Franco in the Spanish Civil War (1936-1939).

Italian dictator Benito Mussolini, German leader Adolf Hitler, interpreter Paul Schmidt, and British prime minister Neville Chamberlain in conference in Munich on September 29, 1938. Chamberlain, who left the meeting convinced that he had outwitted Hitler and prevented a future conflict, found himself proven terribly wrong on September 1, 1939, when the German invasion of Poland signalled the outbreak of World War II.

Germany. France had earlier pledged to defend Czechoslovakia against aggression, and the Soviet Union, the other Czech ally, was not even permitted to attend the Munich Conference.

Munich was to be called an "appeasement" of Hitler. To Stalin it looked like the simple betrayal of an ally. He feared that German aggression would be directed at the Soviet Union and that the Western democracies would not help. He was apprehensive about his country's state of readiness, weakened as it was by the strains of collectivization, industrialization, and the purges. He wondered whether Russia could resist a German attack, or if his regime would collapse.

Stalin decided to open communications with Hitler. At this time, Hitler was making his own plans for the invasion of Poland. A pact with the Soviet Union would avoid a war on two fronts.

A German delegation arrived in Moscow on August 23, 1939. All night long Stalin and Molotov conferred with the German diplomats. In the morning a public treaty of friendship and non-aggression between the two countries was agreed on. There was a secret protocol dividing eastern Europe and the Baltic states into areas of influence. Germany would take western Poland, Russia the eastern part.

The news of the pact shocked the world. Communist parties in other countries felt betrayed and

Adolf Hitler and Field Marshal Gerd von Runstedt discuss the German invasion of France in June 1940. Von Runstedt, who later commanded the southern group of German armies in the Soviet Union, was one of the few German generals who realized within months of the June 1941 invasion that the attempt to conquer the Soviets would never succeed.

disgraced. That the pact hurt world communism bothered Stalin not one bit. At a champagne party after the night's work, he offered a toast to Hitler, saying, "I know how much the German nation loves its Fuhrer."

On September 1, 1939, Hitler's troops attacked Poland. Two days later, Britain and France declared war on Germany and World War II began. The Soviet Union had avoided involvement, but it took its portion of victimized Poland later in the month.

Stalin now strived to strengthen his position. He compelled the Baltic states to grant military bases to Soviet forces. But when he demanded bases in Finland, the Finns refused. The Soviet Union then invaded Finland.

At first, to Stalin's humiliation, the Red Army was rebuffed. Because of the purges of Soviet military leaders, the Soviet forces had difficulty overcoming the much smaller nation. Hitler, watching closely, concluded that the Soviet Union would be a

> To the Chancellor of the German Reich, A. Hitler: *I thank you for the letter. I hope that the German-Soviet non-aggression pact will mark a decided turn for the better in the political relations between our countries.*
> —JOSEPH STALIN
> writing on August 22, 1939

American cartoonist Clifford Berryman's astute comment on the non-aggression treaty contracted between Germany and the Soviet Union on August 23, 1939.

WONDER HOW LONG THE HONEYMOON WILL LAST?

A tank of the German Condor Legion in action against anti-fascist forces in Spain in 1937. Stalin directed his efforts in Spain not only against the fascists and their German and Italian allies, but also against "Trotskyite" elements among the anti-fascist Spanish communists. Stalin's idea of "fraternal support" proved fatal to many Spanish leftists who had thought him their most reliable ally.

pushover for the German army.

Stalin's consternation grew in 1940 when the Nazis quickly rolled over northern Europe and France. Nonetheless, he kept the trade agreements he had made with Germany. The Soviet Union supplied Nazi Germany with oil, iron ore, cotton and other strategic materials that kept the German war machine going. In return, the Soviets were to receive manufactured goods from Germany. These were often late. But Stalin was so eager to keep the non-aggression pact alive that he only made weak protests.

In his fear of arousing Hitler's ire, Stalin did not use the time well to increase preparedness. In spite of warnings that Hitler was planning to invade the Soviet Union, few specific precautions were taken. Artillery units and airfields near the border were not even camouflaged.

The only positive step that Stalin took was the Neutrality Pact with Japan. Japan had occupied Manchuria, and in the 1930s there were border skirmishes between Japanese and Soviet troops. Stalin, too, wished to avoid a two-front war, and reached a non-aggression pact with Japan in April 1941.

Stalin, who was rarely seen in public, took the unusual step of accompanying the Japanese diplomats to the railway station to bid them farewell. At the station, he embraced both the Japanese ambassador and the German military attaché, telling the German, "We will remain friends with you in any event." Less than two months later, Germany and the Soviet Union were at war.

In the early morning hours of June 22, 1941, German troops, planes, and tanks invaded the Soviet Union. It was an enormous attack, on a 2,000-mile front from the Baltic to the Black Sea. Hitler had assembled the most powerful army in history for the task. It was a three-pronged attack, with German army groups moving toward Lenin-

Vyacheslav Molotov, the Soviet commissar for foreign affairs, signs the Soviet-German non-aggression treaty in Moscow on August 23, 1939.

grad, toward Moscow, and into the Ukraine.

The object of the invasion was to destroy the Red Army in huge battles of annihilation. The Nazis advanced rapidly on all fronts. Hundreds of Soviet aircraft were destroyed and defensive fortifications captured. On the first day, Brest-Litovsk, a key to the Soviet defenses, fell, and the Soviet units that were surrounded radioed in vain for instructions. Hitler boasted, "We have only to kick in the door and the whole rotten structure will come crashing down." This had been Stalin's fear as well.

Stalin, who had made himself premier a month earlier, remained silent. The news of the invasion was announced by Molotov. Nikita Khrushchev, Stalin's successor, claimed later that the dictator reacted to the invasion with "nervousness and hysteria."

But Stalin recovered and presented to his people a face of iron determination. Whatever his private doubts and fears, for the rest of the war he never faltered in publicly calling for complete victory. He addressed the Soviet people by radio on July 3, calling for a "scorched earth" policy. Everything

Field Marshal Carl Gustaf von Mannerheim (1867-1951), the Finnish soldier who led his country's forces against the Soviet invasion in 1939. The Red Army suffered a severe loss of prestige when the impetus of its attack in southern Finland foundered against the Finnish army's tough defense of the fortifications known as the Mannerheim Line.

that could be useful to the enemy was to be destroyed before it could be captured. The precious fruits of collectivization and industrialization, gained at such an enormous human cost, were to be sacrificed for victory.

Yet the Nazis drove on. By the end of September Leningrad had been besieged. Much of the Ukraine had been overrun. Here, many people greeted the Germans as liberators. At Kiev, in the Ukraine, the Germans claimed 600,000 prisoners. Stalin ordered the destruction of the Dnieper Dam, the showpiece of the first Five Year Plan. Only at Smolensk, in mid-July, did the Germans meet serious opposition. But the city fell.

Russia's situation was critical. Two and one-half million men had been captured or killed. The losses in material were also enormous—18,000 tanks and 14,000 planes. By the end of November Soviet industrial production was cut in half.

In October the Germans advanced to within 30 miles of Moscow itself. Hitler ordered that the Kremlin was to be blown up to signify the overthrow of Bolshevism. About half the city's 4 million people

Finnish ski troops conduct a patrol near the Soviet border in December 1939. Finland's defense chief, Field Marshal Mannerheim, finally persuaded his government to accept the Soviet surrender terms on March 13, 1940. Mannerheim had begun his military career as an officer in the Russian army, resigning in 1917 and returning to Finland, where he ruthlessly suppressed the Bolshevik-engineered Finnish Workers' Republic.

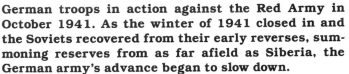

German troops in action against the Red Army in October 1941. As the winter of 1941 closed in and the Soviets recovered from their early reverses, summoning reserves from as far afield as Siberia, the German army's advance began to slow down.

A Soviet army officer poses beside his armored car in the Polish city of Brest-Litovsk in September 1939, as German officers look on. The arrival of Soviet forces in Brest-Litovsk signalled the active conclusion of that clause in the German-Soviet treaty of August 1939 whereby the two countries had agreed to divide Poland.

fled. When most government offices were moved out of the city, many people panicked and tried to leave. Stalin himself remained in the Kremlin, directing the defense of the city.

Three-quarters of the remaining people in Moscow were women and children, because the men had been organized into workers' battalions and sent to the front. A state of siege was declared. All radio sets were confiscated, and trucks with loudspeakers broadcast news of the battles. The civilians fortified the city with tank traps and barricades. Trees were cut down to fuel power plants. Five hundred factories in the area were dismantled and sent to the east.

On the anniversary of the revolution, Stalin reviewed the city's defense units and evoked the Russian past: "Let the manly images of our great

Moscow's Kremlin fortress, the administrative and political center of the Soviet Union. Stalin remained in the Kremlin for much of the time following the German invasion, perhaps assuming, as some historians have suggested, that to have left might have appeared defeatist.

ВСЕ ДЛЯ ПОБЕДЫ!

ФРОНТУ ОТ ЖЕНЩИН СССР

A Soviet propaganda poster from 1942 stresses the important role which women played in war production, thus releasing thousands of men for front-line combat duty.

ancestors . . . inspire you in this war. . . . Death to the German invaders! Long live our glorious country, its freedom, its independence!" Copies of Stalin's speech were printed and dropped into occupied areas. His presence in the Kremlin throughout the war became an inspiration to Russian resistance.

The German advance on Moscow slowed. Twice the Germans stormed the city and were repulsed. Then, on December 6, when the temperature fell to 40° below zero, Stalin gave the order for a counterattack. General Georgi Zhukov was now in charge. In the attack, the Germans were thrown back, retreating more than 100 miles.

The victory spread confidence throughout the country. Stalin encouraged this mood and called for victory in 1942.

The country needed all the confidence it could muster to survive the winter of 1941-42. In besieged Leningrad, the food supply ran low and hundreds of thousands died of starvation. In the occupied territories, conditions were horrendous. The racial doctrines of the Nazis defined Slavs as inferior people, and the occupying troops committed terrible atrocities against both civilians and prisoners of war. Many former collaborators became guerrillas and fought against the Germans.

The Germans continued their advance in new offensives in 1942. The main campaigns were on the southern front, concentrating on the Caucasus with its oil reserves, and the lower Don and Volga region. The fighting around Stalingrad was both critical and fierce. The city became the focus of a titanic clash of wills between two determined and desperate dictators fighting for political and military survival.

By late August the Russian defenders had been pushed back into the heart of the city. The civilian population had been evacuated and the factory workers enlisted in fighting battalions. Each building was mined, sniper nests were constructed, and the order was given: "Not a step back!"

In September, with the city mostly rubble, the Germans controlled most of the city. The fighting grew more desperate. Russian soldiers carrying live hand grenades threw themselves under German tanks. Hand-to-hand fighting went on in the ruins of houses, factories, cellars, and sewers. To conquer a single street cost the Germans more casualties than they had lost in entire countries earlier in the war.

Stalin addressed the garrison by radio on October 5: "I demand that you take every measure. . . . Stalingrad must not be yielded to the enemy." As the besieged defenders clung to an ever-decreasing part of the rubble of Stalingrad, General Zhukov brought up reserve forces at the rear of the German attackers. He struck on November 19, and in four days the tables were turned. The German besiegers were now the besieged.

The Russians drove back the German forces that surrounded the city. By the end of December, the Germans were thrown back more than 100 miles. This maneuver left isolated the German troops inside the city. In a rage, Hitler ordered his commander neither to surrender nor to attempt to break out of the Soviet ring surrounding Stalingrad. But on January 31, 1943, 91,000 men out of an original 300,000 gave up. Stalingrad had held and, with the victory, the spirit of the Soviet people rose.

Stalingrad was Hitler's greatest defeat at that point in the war. And it was a great personal victory for Stalin. He had been active in the military planning, investing all his prestige as ruler of the country in the city's defense. He had pitted himself against Hitler and won. He made himself a marshal of the army in March 1943.

Stalingrad was a crucial battle in the war against Hitler. Germany was losing manpower in the Soviet Union at a rate it could not replace. The myth of the invincibility of the German army lay in the rubble of Stalingrad.

The war brought about a change in Stalin's relationship to the nation. The initial weakness of Soviet defenses showed the damage caused by the upheavals of the 1930s. In response, Stalin ordered many military officers and civilians released

Georgi Zhukov (1896-1974), the Soviet general who led the first major counterattack against the German invaders in December 1941. Zhukov went on to lead the Soviet forces which crushed the Germans at Stalingrad and Leningrad between October 1942 and January 1943.

from prison camps. The propaganda about treachery within the party stopped. With a much clearer threat from Germany, there was no more news of Trotskyite plots.

The greatest change was a resurgence of Russian nationalism. The people responded to Stalin's appeal to the greatness of the Russian past. Given the beastliness of the Nazi racial policies, many found that Russia was worth fighting for. A former tsarist general told a German commander, "If only you had come twenty years ago we should have welcomed you with open arms. But now it's too late. . . . Now we are fighting for Russia and in that cause we are all united."

Stalin identified himself with that Russian past. Originally a Georgian, he fused himself with Russian aspirations now that victory seemed possible. Stalin in the Kremlin became the symbol of Russian victory. Millions of Russian soldiers died with

Relief workers search through the ruins of a Moscow school destroyed by German bombs in October 1941. In November that same year Stalin made a speech in which he compared Hitler's regime to that of the tsars of Russia, thus exhibiting his tendency to relate the urgent and unprecedented issues of the present to events of the revolutionary past.

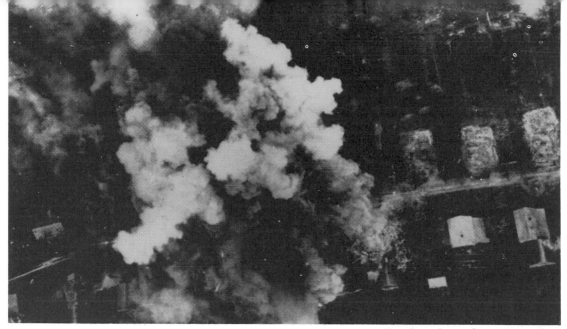

Smoke rises from Russian positions on the Leningrad front bombed by German aircraft in October 1941. The first disastrous months of the German invasion almost broke Stalin, who responded to the desperate situation by drinking heavily and making life impossible for his staff.

The ruins of Minsk in 1941, following the German blitz on the city in the opening stages of the invasion. Minsk remained in German hands until July 3, 1944, when armored forces under General Rotmistrov drove into the city, concluding a tough military action which had netted almost 100,000 German prisoners.

Field Marshal Friedrich von Paulus, the German commander at Stalingrad who surrendered to the Soviet forces surrounding the city on January 31, 1943. Few of the 91,000 German prisoners taken at Stalingrad ever returned to their homeland, since the Soviets treated German captives as barbarically as the Germans did Soviet prisoners. According to some reports, 400,000 German prisoners died in Soviet camps between February and April of 1942, mainly of cold and starvation.

the words "For country and for Stalin" on their lips.

Other traditions were revived. Ranks were introduced in the army. The officer corps was covered with honors. The Orthodox Church was rehabilitated despite its criticisms of the Bolshevik regime. The head of the church was invited to the Kremlin for a long, friendly interview with Stalin. Even the *Internationale* was dropped as the national anthem and replaced by a more nationalistic song. Books and movies celebrated Russian history under the tsars.

After Stalingrad, more than two years of hard fighting lay ahead. In July 1943 the Germans launched their last major invasion but were decisively thrown back. The German front began to collapse. By the end of 1943 the Soviet armies had regained two-thirds of the territory that had been taken. The following year would see the raising of the siege of Leningrad and the entrance of Soviet forces into parts of eastern Europe. They were poised to begin an onslaught on Hitler's Fortress Europe.

When the Soviet Union was invaded in 1941, both Britain and the United States offered assistance in the form of arms and material. Although there were many Allied powers fighting Germany, Prime Minister Winston Churchill of Britain, President Franklin D. Roosevelt of the United States, and Stalin became known as the Big Three. Several times they met in person to discuss strategy.

Churchill was vehemently anticommunist, but he welcomed the help of the Soviets against the Nazi threat. Roosevelt, on the other hand, had extended United States diplomatic recognition to the Soviet Union and granted loans and supplies when they were most needed.

Stalin had two basic objectives in his relationships with his allies. He wanted a guarantee of the borders of 1941, giving him the areas he seized after the non-aggression pact. This matter was put off until later in the war, because his second objective was more pressing: an Allied invasion of France

As the tide of war turns against Hitler in 1943, German troops salvage a single tank from a barn set ablaze by Soviet guerrillas. In 1942 Stalin had acknowledged the paramount importance of the military commanders by declaring their decisions binding upon the political commissars attached to the Red Army. This was a most unusual move for a dictator who had purged his armed forces of their most capable officers during the 1930s.

Stalin's son Jacob, photographed in a German prison camp in 1943, shortly before he was shot by guards whom he had begged to kill him. The details of Jacob's death, discovered by Allied forces in Germany in 1945, were never disclosed to Stalin.

that would open a second front and divert Hitler's forces away from Russia.

Churchill first visited Stalin in Moscow in August 1942. This was a time of great stress for Stalin, with German armies advancing on Stalingrad. Churchill had a particularly unpleasant task to perform, which he likened to "carrying a large lump of ice to the North Pole." He had to tell Stalin the promised second front would not occur in 1942. The following dialogue took place:

Churchill: We have reached the conclusion . . . I find it difficult to talk about this, but . . .

Stalin: There are no people with weak nerves here, Prime Minister.

Churchill: The invasion of Europe is impossible this year . . .

Stalin: That is to say that the English and American leaders renounce the solemn promise made to us. . . .

Churchill was able to reveal to Stalin the Allied plans for an invasion of northern Africa, held by the Germans. Churchill was amazed at Stalin's quick grasp of the military plans. Churchill later said, "Very few people alive could have comprehended in so few minutes [the plan]. He saw it all in a flash."

By the time Stalin met Churchill and Roosevelt in Teheran in November 1943, the Soviet Union was on the offensive against Germany. The outcome of the war from the Soviet viewpoint was no

СОРЕВНУЙТЕСЬ НА ЛУЧШУЮ ПОМОЩЬ ФРОНТУ!

The caption to this 1942 Soviet propaganda poster reads: "Follow this worker's example. Produce more for the front!" While the Soviets did manage vastly to increase domestic production of war materials during the conflict, their effort received much assistance in the form of weapons and equipment provided by Great Britain and the United States.

Joseph Stalin receives the ceremonial sword which was presented to him by Winston Churchill on behalf of King George VI of England at the Teheran Conference in 1943. The sword honored the Soviet victory at Stalingrad.

longer in doubt. Stalin was in a particularly strong position, because he knew his partners wanted his help against Japan.

At Teheran, Roosevelt promised an invasion of France in the spring. Stalin agreed to enter the war against Japan when the war in Europe was over. His other major success at Teheran was in persuading Roosevelt and Churchill to agree to his definition of the eastern boundary of Poland.

With these decisions made in his favor, Stalin relaxed. He got on quite well with Roosevelt, who said, "I believe he is truly representative of the heart and soul of Russia; and I believe that we are going to get along very well with him and the Russian people—very well indeed."

On behalf of the king of England, Churchill

presented Stalin with a ceremonial sword honoring the Soviet victory at Stalingrad. Roosevelt reported that he saw tears in Stalin's eyes as he accepted the sword in the name of the Russian people.

Stalin could be charming to the Allied leaders when he chose, but his private evaluation of them was different. He said to a Yugoslavian official, "Churchill is the kind who, if you don't watch him, will slip a kopeck [coin] out of your pocket! By God, a kopeck out of your pocket! And Roosevelt? Roose-

Joseph Stalin with America's President Roosevelt and Britain's Premier Churchill in Teheran in 1943. Many historians believe that Roosevelt's acceptance of Stalin's offer of accommodation in the Soviet embassy for the duration of the conference was unwise, since Stalin's security men had installed many listening devices throughout the president's quarters.

Premier Churchill, President Roosevelt, and Generalissimo Stalin at the Yalta Conference in February 1945. Early in the proceedings Stalin raised the issue which he considered central to the whole meeting—to minimize the possibility of conflict between the three major powers (Great Britain, the United States, and the Soviet Union) once the war with Germany had been brought to a conclusion.

velt is not like that. He dips in his hand only for the bigger coins. But Churchill? Churchill—even for a kopeck!"

The three met again at Yalta in February 1945, when the war was almost over. They agreed to the postwar division of Germany into zones controlled by their three countries and France. They agreed on free elections in all the occupied countries of Europe, including Poland. Stalin affirmed his intention to enter the war against Japan.

The last major Allied conference was at Potsdam, Germany, in July 1945. Roosevelt had died in April, and the new American president, Harry Truman, represented the United States. The Big Three were now in the position of conquerors of a defeated Germany. The Russians had led the final assault on Berlin, which fell May 2.

Truman was later to say of Stalin, "I like old Uncle Joe Stalin. He is a fine man, but he is a prisoner of the politburo. You could make an agreement with him, but the other people on the politburo would not let him keep his word."

There were tears in his [Stalin's] eyes. I saw them myself. He bowed from the hips swiftly and kissed the sword, a ceremonial gesture of great style which I know was unrehearsed. It was really very magnificent, moving and sincere. He is a very interesting man. They say he is a peasant from one of the least progressive parts of Russia, but let me tell you he had an elegance of manner which none of the rest of us had.
—FRANKLIN D. ROOSEVELT

Marshal Semën Timoshenko, the brilliant Soviet officer whom Stalin appointed people's commissar for defense in 1940 and subsequently assigned to the Moscow-Smolensk region of the central front following the German invasion of 1941. In the early stages of the invasion, when the Red Army was reeling before the German onslaught, Timoshenko managed to maneuver 500,000 troops to safety when German forces had almost overwhelmed them.

Churchill and Stalin with President Harry Truman at the Potsdam Conference in July 1945. With Hitler defeated, the collapse of Japan imminent, and the Red Army in occupation of much of eastern Europe, Stalin bargained much harder at Potsdam than he had at any previous talks. In the opinion of many historians, Stalin emerged from the negotiations with a tremendous political advantage over his allies.

At Potsdam, Truman revealed the success of the American effort to develop an atomic bomb, and the plans to use it on Japan. This caused Stalin to hurry his declaration of war on Japan so that he could share in the spoils of war.

In a victory celebration at the Kremlin in May 1945, Stalin offered a toast to the Russian people, admitting that the government had "made not a few errors. We experienced at moments a desperate situation in 1941-1942. . . . A different people could have said to the government, 'You have failed to justify our expectations. Go away. We shall install another government which will conclude peace with Germany. . . .' The Russian people, however, did not take this path. . . . Thanks to it, to the Russian people, for this confidence."

This was one of Stalin's more honest pronouncements.

German prisoners march through Moscow in 1944. Soviet forces made massive gains in eastern and northern Europe that year, driving the Germans out of Rumania, Hungary, Bulgaria, the Baltic states, and northern Norway. Such advances cleared the way for the final Soviet lunge across Nazi Germany's borders in January 1945.

5

"A Rude Old Man"

The victory over the Nazis was the high point of Stalin's regime. On June 24, 1945, units of the victorious Soviet army paraded through Red Square to honor the architect of the victory as he watched from a balcony on the Kremlin wall. Stalin stood in the rain for hours as his soldiers dropped hundreds of captured German regimental banners at the base of the wall.

With the empires of France and Britain dissolving, the Soviet Union and the United States emerged as the two world superpowers. In contrast to America, which had not been devastated by the fighting, the Soviet Union had lost about 20 million people, civilians and soldiers both, and suffered enormous physical damage as well. In their retreat, the Germans had destroyed everything in their path. Fully one-quarter of all property in the Soviet Union had been lost. Twenty-five million were homeless.

Stalin called on his people for more sacrifices. In 1946 he announced the shift from a looser Russian nationalism to a hard Marxist line. The fourth Five Year Plan began, with emphasis on steel, coal, and oil production.

The United States offered aid to help rebuild Europe through the Marshall Plan. Stalin turned down

British author George Orwell (1903-1950), whose book *Animal Farm*, published in 1945, mercilessly exposed the dangers of Stalinism and became an instant classic. Orwell acquired his contempt for Stalin while fighting the fascists in the Spanish Civil War, when he saw that the Soviets were more concerned with killing Trotskyite communists than with defeating fascism.

Joseph Stalin shortly before his death in 1953. In February 1952 Stalin had finished work on a book entitled *Economic Problems of Socialism in the U.S.S.R.*, perhaps intended to be the last word on the subject. Western historians, however, consider it little more than a rambling monologue which suggests that Stalin lacked the detailed knowledge crucial to the successful treatment of this complex subject.

British airmen celebrate the delivery of the one-millionth ton of supplies to the beleaguered citizens of Berlin in 1949. Supplying the divided city by air became essential in 1948 when Stalin denied the British, American, and French administrations road access to the city through the Soviet section of occupied Germany.

the offer, though he needed the aid badly. He was afraid of losing his economic independence by accepting capitalist aid.

Stalin forced the eastern European countries to decline Marshall Plan aid as well. With his armies occupying most of Europe east of Berlin, Stalin found it easy to disregard the promises of free elections made at Yalta and Potsdam. Governments loyal to Moscow were installed in Poland, Yugoslavia, Czechoslovakia, Bulgaria, Rumania, Albania, and East Germany. In a rare candid moment, Stalin admitted, "A freely elected government in any of these countries would be anti-Soviet, and that we cannot allow." In 1946 Churchill spoke of an "iron curtain" descending over eastern Europe.

Thus began the "cold war" rivalry between the United States and the Soviet Union. Stalin referred privately to President Truman as "the great shopkeeper." Truman could not use troops to liberate eastern Europe, but he extended aid to Greece and Turkey to help them overcome communist rebellions.

Defeated Germany, as agreed at Yalta and Potsdam, had been divided into four sectors. Berlin, the former capital, lay within the Soviet zone, but was administered by the four victorious powers. In 1948 Britain, the United States, and France agreed to combine their zones into West Germany. In response, Stalin cut off access routes to Berlin. Truman ordered an airlift of supplies that kept the city out of Soviet hands. The following year Stalin was forced to back down.

After Stalin received reports of the power of the atomic bombs the United States had dropped on Japan, he ordered Soviet scientists to begin work on a similar bomb. In 1949 the Soviet Union became the second country to develop its own atomic weapon.

Stalin met a surprising setback in Yugoslavia in 1948. With Stalin's aid, the partisan forces of Josip Broz Tito had taken control of the country at the end of World War II. Tito was a communist, but showed a determination to pursue an independent economic policy. He was unwilling to sign the unfavorable trade agreements Moscow was trying to force on his country.

The Russians removed their trade delegation from Yugoslavia and Stalin accused Tito of being "an imperialist spy." He said to Khrushchev, "I will shake my finger—and there will be no more Tito. He will fall." But Tito survived and continued to pursue an independent policy.

The other communist figure who followed his own policy was Mao Tse-tung, the Chinese leader. Stalin's relations with the Chinese communist movement had always been stormy. In the 1920s he had ordered the fledgling party in China to cooperate with Chiang Kai-shek. This decision led to a mass slaughter of communists when Chiang turned on them.

Mao had taken the remnants of the party and built it into a force capable of taking over the world's most populous nation. During World War II Stalin had recognized Chiang's government, and even in the civil war that followed he withheld formal recognition of Mao until just before the final victory in 1949.

Stalin distrusted communist movements that had any independence from him. Mao not only owed little to Stalin, but had also developed his own theory as to how Marxism could be applied in China.

General George Marshall (1880-1959), the American soldier and statesman whose "Marshall Plan," formulated in 1947, provided a blueprint for the economic recovery of Europe from the ravages caused by World War II. Stalin refused all offers of Marshall aid for the Soviet-occupied states of eastern Europe, fearing Western interference in an area which he intended to keep under Soviet domination.

He ruled over a country which, because of its size, could make it a competitor with the Soviet Union for the leadership of world communism.

Privately, Stalin disparaged Mao, calling him a "margarine Marxist" (not the real thing). But when Mao came to Moscow, Stalin could hardly snub the leader of one of the communist "family of nations." Even so, after three months of hard bargaining, Stalin granted Mao only a small loan and a formal alliance. Ironically, Mao was regarded in the West as merely Stalin's puppet.

Stalin's achievements in the war gave further impetus to what his successor called "the cult of personality." After Lenin's death, the other Soviet leaders had played on his memory to keep the loyalty of the people and the party. As Stalin's power grew, the portrayal of him as supreme leader rivalled Lenin's, and then grew to fantastic proportions.

Posters and paintings always showed Stalin as a middle-aged man in the prime of his life, a massive and majestic figure standing head and shoulders above his comrades. Enormous pictures of him were placed on the sides of buildings; innumerable smaller pictures were in virtually every home and office throughout the country.

This 1947 cartoon by Edwin Marcus addressed the uncertainty felt by Western politicians concerning Stalin's probable response to offers of aid for eastern Europe under the terms of the Marshall Plan.

Chiang Kai-shek (1887-1975), the Chinese soldier and nationalist leader with whom Stalin ordered the Chinese communists to collaborate during the 1920s. Despite the fact that Chiang's Kuomintang movement, which Stalin had initially considered useful to Soviet interests in the Far East, slaughtered many Chinese communists in 1926, Stalin continued to recognize Chiang's government until the communists under Mao Tse-tung overthrew the Kuomintang in 1949.

Lion Feuchtwanger was bold enough to ask Stalin about the display in 1937. Stalin "apologized for his workers and peasants, who are too busy with other things to cultivate good taste. . . . He suggested that these are people who have accepted the existing regime rather late and now are trying to prove their loyalty with doubled zeal. Yes, he considers it possible that this could be a plot of wreckers to discredit him. . . . He tolerates all the ballyhoo, he declared, only because he knew what naive joy the festive hubbub gives to its organizers."

Stalin could share the glory with no one else. During the war, he adopted a marshal's uniform and continued to wear it until his death as a reminder of his military glory. Popular generals such

Josip Broz Tito (1892-1980), the Yugoslavian soldier and statesman who so angered Stalin when he refused to sign a series of basically unfavorable trade agreements with the Soviet government. A communist since World War I, when he was a prisoner of war in Russia, Tito established a socialist republic in Yugoslavia in 1945.

as Zhukov were no longer seen in public after the war.

The sorts of tributes he received on his 50th birthday in 1929 grew more preposterous in the years that followed. Stalin was "our beloved father," "our dear guide and teacher," "the greatest leader of all times and of all peoples." The cult and flattery spread to communist parties in other nations.

Poets and musicians composed works to celebrate him and his feats. The Orthodox Patriarch (head of the church) called him "the chosen son of Providence." Virtually every book had to contain some reference to him. Even researchers on scientific and academic topics had to find ways to allude to Stalin's views on the subject, and his ideas on any topic had to be considered.

Stalin became omnipresent. No public place was without his portrait. In movie theaters, backlighted silhouettes of Stalin and Lenin flanked the sides of the screen. Statues of him were carried to the highest mountains and the most remote forests.

In 1951 Stalin signed the order for a massive statue of himself to be erected on the Volga-Don Canal. Thirty-three tons of bronze went into its construction. Two men could lie down on the epaulettes of the thirty-six foot high body.

Though Stalin made few public appearances in later years, the cult made people feel as if he were always present, always watching. In the words of

Mao Tse-tung (1893-1976), the Chinese communist leader whose independent policies earned him Stalin's distrust. The cultural and political differences between the two men became highly apparent during Mao's 1949-1950 Moscow visit. The Chinese leader, as ruler of 600 million people, not unnaturally considered himself Stalin's equal and showed no interest in the junior partner status which the Soviet dictator had hoped to force upon him.

Ilya Ehrenburg, a Soviet writer, "In the minds of millions, Stalin was transformed into a mythical demigod; everyone trembled as they said his name, believed that he alone would save the Soviet Union from invasion and collapse."

Perhaps the height of Stalin's cult was reached by a *Pravda* writer in 1950: "If you meet with difficulties in your work, or suddenly doubt your abilities, think of him, of Stalin, and you will find the confidence you need. If you feel tired in an hour when you should not—think of him, of Stalin, and your work will go well. If you are seeking a correct decision, think of him, of Stalin, and you will find that decision . . . 'Stalin said' —that means the people think so. 'The people said' —that means Stalin thought so."

Stalin also ordered the rewriting of history books and encyclopedias to increase his role in the Revolution and other important events. The work of others was downplayed, or in the case of those

A portrait of Stalin confronts shoppers in Prague, the capital of Czechoslovakia, in 1948. Following the removal of Stalin's body from the Lenin mausoleum in 1961, de-Stalinization became obligatory throughout the Soviet bloc. The dictator's memorial in Prague was so large that, when all attempts to camouflage it failed, the Czech government had it blown up by the military.

Cheering crowds gather in Moscow's Red Square in 1952, celebrating the 35th anniversary of the Russian Revolution. Stalin's speech to the 19th Party Congress in October of that year surprised his audience, since the great dictator spoke approvingly of such concepts as democracy and national independence. Despite Stalin's tone on this occasion, neither democracy nor independence became noticeable features of political life in the Soviet satellite states of eastern Europe.

purged, left out altogether. Even photographs were retouched to show Stalin next to Lenin, with Trotsky removed.

For his official biography, Stalin was not content with the adulation lavished on his career by his own flunkies. According to Khrushchev, Stalin added such items to the book as: "Although he performed his task of leader of the party and the people with consummate skill and enjoyed the unreserved support of the entire Soviet people, Stalin never allowed his work to be marred by the slightest hint of vanity, conceit, or self-adulation." Clearly, flattery was, to Stalin, a drug he could not get enough of.

In his final years, Stalin's mental and physical strength declined, but since the affairs of state revolved around him, everything just had to wait

The map shows the extent of Soviet political mastery in the world at the time of Stalin's death in 1953.

on his decisions. Toward the end, government all but ground to a halt. He slept to midday and worked afternoons and evenings. His behavior was often coarse and irritable. He called himself "a rude old man."

A window in the Kremlin was always kept lighted through the night so that people in the street could see that Stalin was still working tirelessly.

He kept around him a circle of cronies—party and government officials—who might be roused out of bed at any hour to go driving through the city or to eat and drink with Stalin. A Yugoslavian diplomat who often visited Stalin said that Stalin ate enormous quantities of food. The dinners would continue for hours, until four or five in the morning.

Everyone had to pay attention to what Stalin said, for if he discussed affairs of state, his orders had to be carried out the next day. And if he decided to be entertaining, everyone laughed at his jokes and stories. The Yugoslav told of Stalin's playing a phonograph record on which an opera singer was accompanied by a chorus of barking dogs. When the Yugoslav did not quite share in the mirth, Stalin explained, "Well, still it's clever, devilishly clever."

More and more frequently, Stalin spent his time at a country house southwest of Moscow. When he was traveling to and from the Kremlin, the route was guarded by 3000 security agents. His traveling companions went along, in five black limousines with closed window curtains, armor plate, and bullet-proof glass. Stalin rode in a different one of the five cars each time to confuse would-be assassins. No one was allowed to disclose Stalin's whereabouts.

On occasion, Stalin still purged officials, but not on the scale of the 1930s. He liked to encourage rivalries among those close to him to keep them off balance. Everyone lived in fear that Stalin would decide he was not trustworthy.

Then, in January 1953, a sinister headline appeared in *Pravda*:

MISERABLE SPIES AND ASSASSINS MASKING AS PROFESSORS OF MEDICINE

A shudder went through millions of people who noted the similarity to headlines during the purges of the 1930s. The article described "hidden enemies of our people." The State Security agency had uncovered a "terrorist group" of doctors who had attempted to shorten the lives of leading Soviet figures.

Of the nine "enemies" listed, six were Jewish. They were called agents of Zionist and British intelligence.

Stalin's anti-Semitism had grown with his years. In 1952, 25 Jewish writers and intellectuals had been shot. The discovery of new Jewish "enemies," as well as the ominous words, "and others," meant

Lavrenti Beria (1899-1953), the Soviet secret police chief who replaced Nikolai Yezhov in 1938. Responsible for many political murders, Beria was executed by Joseph Stalin's successors shortly after the dictator's death.

to many that the era of the 1930s was to be repeated.

The anxiety was calmed only by the news of Stalin's death a month and a half later. On the morning of March 6, 1953, citizens of the Soviet Union were told: "The heart of Joseph Vissariono-vich Stalin, Lenin's comrade-in-arms and inspired continuator of his work, wise leader and educator of the Communist Party and the Soviet people, has stopped beating."

Huge crowds assembled in Red Square outside the Kremlin. Funeral music blared from loudspeakers in the cities and in the villages. Many wept and were apprehensive about life without Stalin. The

Soviet troops escort the gun carriage bearing Stalin's body to the Lenin mausoleum on March 9, 1953. Hundreds of Soviet citizens had died during the previous three days, trampled to death in the vast crowds which had gathered in Moscow to pay their last respects to the leader who had ruled them so harshly for so long.

Joseph Stalin's portrait keeps the best orthodox communist company on a public building in Gori, Georgia, during the 1960s. While images of Stalin disappeared into relative obscurity throughout the Soviet Union and its satellite states during the Khrushchev era, the citizens of Stalin's native land continued to revere him.

Soviet novelist Mikhail Sholokhov wrote on Stalin's death:

Farewell, Father!

That sudden and terrible feeling of having become an orphan!

But others had different feelings. A student told a friend, "I have been locked in my room, so as not to betray myself. I am so happy." In the labor camps, still filled with Stalin's enemies, there was rejoicing. An inmate at Vorkuta camp said, "I have been here for 19 years and this is the first good news I have heard."

Long lines of people waited for a glimpse of Stalin's

body, and there was a state funeral on March 9. But then a strange thing began to happen. Stalin's name was gradually dropped from the newspapers. The group leadership that succeeded him did not refer to him. On April 4, *Pravda* announced that the "doctors' conspiracy" had never existed.

When Khrushchev assumed the leadership, he expanded the de-Stalinization process. At the 20th party congress in 1956, Khrushchev gave a long speech denouncing and explaining the crimes of Stalin. He admitted that many victims of the purges were innocent. The speech was never published in the Soviet press, but word of it was spread.

Stalin's body was taken from the grand tomb it shared with Lenin and reburied under the Kremlin wall. The statues and monuments to him gradually disappeared. Today, only his native village of Gori, Georgia, has a major shrine to his memory.

The Soviet people still have not come to terms with the memory of Stalin. During his rule, the country changed from a backward peasant society to a powerful industrialized nation, one of the world's two superpowers. Under his leadership, the Soviet people fought on the winning side of the greatest war in history.

But these real accomplishments came at an enormous cost. A whole generation had been decimated by purges, repression, and war. He had hurt the scientific and cultural life of the nation. His policies muzzled some of its most creative artists, writers, and thinkers.

In the name of justice and equality, Stalin imposed a system of rigid repression and denied fundamental rights and dignity to his own people. Can the achievements ever begin to justify the horrible human cost?

Let the answer be given by a Soviet poet, Yevgeny Yevtushenko:

Double, triple the guard
around the tomb!
So that Stalin may never
get out, nor the past
with Stalin!

A portrait of Joseph Stalin dating from the 1930s, presenting an image of benevolence at a time when Stalin's security services were engaged in killing millions of Soviet citizens.

Chronology

Dec. 21, 1879	Born Joseph Vissarionovich Dzugashvili, in Gori, Georgia
1898	Joins Georgian organization of Marxists
1901	Joins Russian Social Democratic Labor Party
	Goes underground and takes the name "Koba"
Dec. 1905	Meets Lenin for the first time, at Bolshevik conference in Tammerfors, Finland
1907	Meets Trotsky for the first time
Feb. 1912	Stalin becomes member of Bolshevik central committee
1913	Stalin arrested and sentenced to exile in Siberia
March 25, 1917	Stalin arrives in Petrograd after February Revolution
Oct. 23, 1917	Stalin appointed a member of the politburo
Nov. 7, 1917	November Revolution begins
Nov. 9, 1917	Stalin appointed commissar for nationalities
March 24, 1919	Stalin marries Nadezhda Alliluyeva
April 1922	Stalin appointed general secretary of the Communist Party
1925—27	Ousts rivals from party leadership and consolidates position as dictator
1928	Stalin inaugurates first Five Year Plan
1934	Stalin initiates the Great Purge following the assassination of Sergei Kirov
Aug. 23, 1939	Stalin concludes non-aggression pact with Nazi Germany
June 22, 1941	Germany invades the Soviet Union
Nov. 28—Dec. 1, 1943	Stalin attends the Teheran Conference
Feb. 4—12, 1945	Stalin attends the Yalta Conference
May 2, 1945	Soviet forces take Berlin
July 17—Aug. 2, 1945	Stalin attends the Potsdam Conference
1952	Stalin prepares new purge
March 6, 1953	Soviet citizens informed that Stalin is dead

Further Reading

Bortoli, Georges. *The Death of Stalin.* New York: Praeger Publishers, 1975.

Conquest, Robert. *The Great Terror.* New York: Macmillan, 1968.

Crankshaw, Edward. *Khrushchev Remembers.* trans. and ed. by Strobe Talbott. Boston: Little, Brown, 1970.

Deutscher, Isaac. *Stalin: A Political Biography.* New York: Oxford University Press, 1967.

Djilas, Milovan. *Conversations with Stalin.* New York: Harcourt, Brace & World, 1962.

Dmytryshyn, Basil. *U.S.S.R., A Concise History.* New York: Charles Scribner's Sons, 1978.

Grey, Ian. *Stalin: Man of History.* New York: Doubleday, 1979.

Medvedev, Roy A. *Let History Judge.* New York: Alfred A. Knopf, 1971.

Payne, Robert. *The Rise and Fall of Stalin.* New York: Simon and Schuster, 1965.

Riasanovsky, Nicholas V. *A History of Russia.* New York: Oxford University Press, 1984.

Tucker, Robert C. *Stalin as Revolutionary 1879–1929.* New York: W. W. Norton, 1973.

Ulam, Adam B. *Stalin, the Man and His Era.* New York: Viking Press, 1973.

Warth, Robert D. *Joseph Stalin.* New York: Twayne Publishers, 1969.

Wolfe, Bertram D. *Three Who Made a Revolution.* New York: Delta Books, 1964.

Index

Dorothy and Thomas Hoobler have written many histories for young people. Their book *The Trenches: Fighting on the Western Front in World War I* was named a "Best Children's Book of the Year" by *School Library Journal.* They live in New York City with their daughter.

Arthur M. Schlesinger, jr. taught history at Harvard for many years and is currently Albert Schweitzer Professor of the Humanities at City University of New York. He is the author of numerous highly praised works in American history and has twice been awarded the Pulitzer Prize. He served in the White House as special assistant to Presidents Kennedy and Johnson.